A
Passionfruit
as Big as
the Ritz

A Passionfruit as Big as the Ritz

BILL POWELL

Esquival Press

Published by Esquival Press, Cambridge

First published 2025

ISBN 978-1-03690-803-4

A CIP catalogue record for this book is available from the British Library

Printed and bound in the United Kingdom by Short Run Press, Exeter

Editors: Anna Crutchley, Bettina Starke and Ros Horton
Design/Typography: Dale Tomlinson (Typeset in Ravenscar)
Photography: Lotte Attwood

Contents

Preamble

BILL POWELL

What happened to the snows of yesteryear, Harry?

Huge thanks to Anna and Bettina for their patience in reading a raft of my old travel articles, mostly from *The Times*, *The Telegraph* and *The Observer*, to make this little collection. And I am not forgetting Harry Bowker, a senior reporter for the *St Neots Advertiser* in the 1950s who probably saved me from an early, humiliating end to my journalistic career.

At the time, I was an apprentice reporter on the *Hunts Post*, and my task of a Saturday was to cover the soccer fixture for Eynesbury Rovers. At that time, it seems, I would have been principally interested in medieval French poetry and not at all in lower league footie, so I found it difficult to focus on whatever might be going on pitchside. During the game, if there was an incident, a kerfuffle, or if someone had been booked for some infringement, I would turn to my older colleague for enlightenment: 'What happened, Harry?' Without Harry's kind forbearance and his brilliant summaries, shamelessly copied by me, my reporting career might have been over almost before it had begun, there in the creosote imbued Press enclosure at the Eynesbury Rovers home ground.

You will not be surprised to learn that in my later life there have been many occasions when I have looked in vain for a Harry Bowker, a kindly presence who could explain to me what on earth was going on... *mais où sont les neiges d'antan** – or what, indeed might have happened to the snows of yesteryear.

**Ballade des dames du temps jadis*, François Villon, 16th century

Windy City

Walking away from a Cambridge multi-storey car-park and heading towards Trumpington Street, I experience a ghostly tremor of expectation which is nothing to do with the proximity of Fitzbillies cake shop and their famously sticky Chelsea buns. I'm in magical Downing Street, looking up at the bronze and iron curlicues and extravagant Victorian stonework and I'm going back in time. The Chelsea bun and the coffee will have to wait. I am six again, and on my way to see the pickled man.

Summer trippers to Cambridge, and these days there are more than three and a half million of them, usually spend their day videoing college walls and being poled along the Cam for extortionate fees. They gladden the hearts of ice cream hawkers and purveyors of official University baseball caps and hardly ever find their way to the real wonderland of Downing Street. Here, University teaching museums house everything from fossils to fetishes to flints, the sort of academic booty that can only be accumulated by a couple of hundred years of empire.

I dodge the niggling east wind that is funnelling along from St Andrew's Street and make for the cosy gloom of the Zoology Museum. On the way it occurs to me that it is only at this time of year, when the shock-wave of mass tourism has receded, that Cambridge can be seen at its best. When the punters are gone and the East Anglian sky is lowered by a few notches and the Fens start to seep into town, Cambridge becomes itself again. Even the gargoyles perk up.

At the museum I ask if they still have a corpse in formaldehyde hanging about. It used to loom horribly (I add helpfully) from a glass tank at the end of a dark corridor and was much wondered-at by trespassing boys like me.

That sounds all very Damien Hirst they reply, but no – there are no human corpses here, preserved or not. It wouldn't be PC and besides, relatives might sue.

The museum still has the 20-foot tapeworm in its preserving jar (plus a little sediment collected over the intervening years) and the whale skeleton swimming through cobwebs high overhead. I would have appreciated, back then, in the age of catapults and short woollen trousers, today's entrance display featuring the world's biggest recorded wasps' nest, the skeleton of an extinct moa and the jaw of a 700,000-year-old mammoth. Wow!

Across the road, the museums of Geology, Archaeology and Anthropology turn out to be much less dark and mothbally than I remember. Cricket-ball size shrunken heads with sewn-up lips no longer grimace from the cabinets, and the smoke-dried human hands that Plains Indians were wont to hang from their war ponies are banished, but my mates and I (no mean re-cyclers of found materials ourselves in those days) would still be able to pay big respect to the native Australian arrowhead makers who chipped exquisite points from the broken glass insulators of outback telegraph lines!

Gone are the high cabinets and drawers like mahogany ziggurats and labels in faded copperplate Latin. The museums are earnestly kid-friendly, yet some of the magic I remember is probably gone the way of the velociraptor (a plastic version of which you can now buy after looking around the Sedgwick fossil collection). Modern ideas of safety, not to mention the fact that a new research institute is now in the way, mean that the late Curator Dr Geoffrey Bushnell's annual demonstrations of spear-throwing out on the grass are unlikely to be reinstated. And a scruffy six-year-old peeking into an office today is not likely to be asked by a distinguished lecturer, as I once was asked, to venture an opinion about a rare Assyrian seal-stone.

'Not many colleagues would agree with me, of course,' the late Miles Burkitt had said, absentmindedly looking down from his cluttered desk and handing me the mysterious find, 'but I think this can't be a day younger than 4,000 years.

'What do you think?'

A Good Day Out

Two (or three) wheels good, four wheels bad.

A hot day in the Suffolk countryside. There's a shimmer over soft tar on the winding lane. A barrister from London wipes his brow, changes down gear on his custom-built tricycle and delivers his opinion in a professional, matter-of-fact way: 'The drivers should be flogged and their filthy cars destroyed with pickaxes or fire, whichever method is cheapest for the taxpayer.'

This is the 14th annual ride of the Veteran Cycle Club, and a group of us have just been shouted at by a youngster in a four-wheel drive monster who told us to 'Get the bleep out of the bleeping road you bunch of bleepheads,' before tossing a drink can our way and roaring off. Now the peace of summer in the English countryside has returned. Feathers have been ruffled, but not too much. Cyclists, I am discovering, are used to being regarded by drivers as (at best) inconvenient survivors from some unimaginable Dark Age Before The Car.

I fall in beside a beautiful Golden Sunbeam roadster from the 1920s and the owner tells me that car driver aggro towards cyclists is worse since the beginning of the present fad for flash four-wheel drive vehicles. Interestingly, he blames manufacturers for pandering to antisocial machismo among the drink can-hurling classes, and concludes, 'A sort of vulgar need to impress and to oppress is inherent in the designs.' My impression of the can-thrower's vehicle had been of adrenaline-inspiring pink paintwork and a logo of sorts on the back depicting (I swear) copulating rhinos. If someone had asked me, I'd have said the whole rig looked like a Rottweiler's breakfast.

We are 45 cyclists strung out in gossipy groups. The bikes range from classic British racers from the '50s right back to solid-tyred originators of the species from the 1880s. It's apparent that enormous numbers of shed-hours have gone into restorations, and much specialist information gets traded on this ride: a pair of Lauterwasser handlebars for a '30s light roadster? No problem! Here's a clockmaker from Saffron Walden who can construct perfect copies of extinct cork hand grips, and another enthusiast who is proposing to make his own tyres. This, I decided as I sprint along on my 30-year-old Holdsworth Mistral through the heady summer air, must represent an unexpected survival from the days when British engineering was learned at the Great Meccano Polytechnic under the kitchen table.

In those days, gone with the grey woollen shorts, cold lino and the admiration, Britishers didn't mind being regarded as dull footlers by foreigners unlikely to know their Whitworth from their BSF. Didn't we assume that other nations had failed to develop cash and character to the neglect of The Shed? Shed talk, with nitpicking and shameless coveting of other people's equipment, gives our ride an abrasive buzz: this is a boozeless cocktail party on wheels.

Ranging over about 50 miles of deepest Cambridgeshire and Suffolk, the party will go on all day, fuelled by the coffee stop at Six Mile Bottom, a pub lunch at Dalham and, best of all, a definitive tea in the church hall at Balsham.

George the GI's latest acquisition – a wife – is commented upon ('that's why he's been restoring the old tandem!'), British Rail comes in for a lot of stick over its increasingly grudging attitude to the carrying of bikes ('BR is definitively cycle-phobic'), and my conversational end is kept up with the story of how I got lost on the way, became a member for a day of a social club and discovered the Chaucerian Knight. Having missed the start from a Sainsbury's car park in Cambridge I'd set off at a great pace on what was supposed to be a short cut. Hours later I realised that I was lost at the lunch-stop pub at Dalham, wherever that was, which would stop serving at any minute.

A large hut loomed out of a hedgerow; a sign said 'Westley Waterless'. I leaned my bike against a brick wall and with serendipitous instinct found myself entering the bar of the village social club. Vicky (God bless her!) signed me in as a temporary member ten minutes before closing time; between fruit machine and pool table and conversations with an earringed boy from the Lego Generation, I clutched my pint thankfully and ate my crisps.

Up a track, not far off from the social club, near an old pond where ducklings compete for *lebensraum* with imperishable plastic rubbish, in a squat and ancient church, lies Sir John de Creke, a contemporary – and even, it has been suggested, the original – of Chaucer's Knight. Fine brasses of Sir John and his wife, Lady Alyne. My reverie was disturbed by *Greensleeves* performed on the chimes of an ice-cream van – by the way, what should it be for ice-cream vans? Pickaxes or fire? Or something really unpleasant? I hot-peddled off to catch up with the column.

When I came upon them, going against the wind in south Cambridgeshire, gossip was rife concerning some members who, not content with going by a modified route, were wanting to form their own organisation! For riders of Rudge-Whitworths only! Heavens! I had already interviewed the appropriately named Mr Bond, their leader and, presently, notable Rudge-Whitworth expert. He was a recent convert to old cycles, he said, via old motorcycles and blowlamps.

His drinking mate John (1950s Mal Rees racer) from the Waggon and Horses at Milton – this pub contingent even brought their own landlady – kept hissing in my ear, 'Ask him what the badge stands for... go on.'

Mr Bond's lapel sported what must have been a prime example of the shed technologist's art: a perfect, brightly polished brooch which was in outline an old-fashioned blowlamp, bearing initials BS. I suspected that it stood for Blowlamp Society, and I also suspected that John and the rest of them would have found it quite amusing. I forbore to ask about the badge. Let 'em make their own entertainment, I always say. A reporter must stick with the job. As when Petra the language student, from Cologne, was bending over her flat tyre, pink and flabbergasted, and a BSA rider looked me straight in the eye and said: 'I think she's got a Continental valve there.' I pretended not to hear. As I saw it, my duty was to get to Balsham as soon as possible and report on the tea.

I passed George and his Missus on their tandem, and Lionel on his 19th-century penny-farthing. 'Whatever you do, don't call it a penny-farthing' he said, from up there, 'It's an Ordinary.' John Skevington's 1886 Marlborough tricycle died away nobly behind me, and I hurried past Birmingham Chapter's Crypto Bantam, a front-wheel pedalled contraption rescued from the cycle evolution's reject-box.

Some wag called after my hurrying back that I was a dead cert to be King of the Tea Stop Stage and to win the Gannet Jersey.

There was no sign of the Rudge-Whitworth schismatics, and a whole posse from the main group had been misdirected by a lady Volvo driver. They would end up enduring an extra 14 miles of separation from the legendary tea spread put on by Balsham's church ladies.

Three Fraser Nash BMW sports cars from the 1930s went by in great style and received friendly waves. As I whizzed by Tom, the Barrister, I wondered how these cars would fare under his novel legislation. 'For the purpose of the proposed new Act' he said, looking after these beauties as Mr Toad might have done, 'they would not be regarded as cars as such…I suggest they would come into the category of, say, three-wheelers that have a usable spare.'

It was like being aboard the *Marie Celeste*, in the church hall; not a soul there, but everything in place. Cakes and sandwiches piled up under cloths, steaming tea urns, trestle tables covered in linen and with flower arrangements in the centre of each one. Surely this was the female equivalent of Shed Technology? A unique collection of delicacies lovingly hand made by the women of Balsham: cakes, buns and rolls such as you would never find in the shop; creations that had the power to stir fragrant memories. Was Proust a cyclist?

Soon the perspiring world would burst in and this tasty little universe would be gone for ever. Angel cakes, Florentines, sausages in puff-pastry, egg and cress sandwiches and all.

Which was exactly what happened a few moments later.

And I joined the demolition as swinishly as anyone.

Dead and Never Called Me Quetzalcoatl!

He was as bald as an oven-ready snipe and about the same size, and he was not a happy little parrot. An old Mayan woman dressed in the traditional embroidered *huipil* of Yucatan, had him tied by his foot to a lump of wood.

A patient, shawl-wrapped pyramid, squatting in truck-tyre sandals and surmounted by a straw hat, she had probably walked since before dawn to get to Merida market from one of the villages towards Quintana Roo. I guessed the fledgling had been found along the way. The woman's wares, a few peppers, tomatoes and jungle fruits, were arranged in tiny piles on the ground and I could have bought out her entire stock for about 50 cents.

For the parrot she wanted 16 pesos – in those days a whole US dollar! And what's more she knew she was going to get it. I was that day's good fortune, a crazy rich Gringo sent by a luck-spirit or the magical Black Virgin of Guadeloupe.

Twenty-five years ago in Mexico – before the cult of sun worship was re-packaged and sold to tourist congregations from Acapulco to Cancun, before new developer-priests had their hands on the country's great heart – an American dollar was an almighty lot of dinero.

The whole Merida market thought I was nuts. But Harry the parrot became mine. What a find! To him I was Lord of all the Parrots, or a cross between his Mum and Quetzalcoatl, the Rainbringer, so we got on just fine. There's nothing like being adored.

Also, there was something generously wild and, well, tropical, about Harry's character that was irresistible to a refugee from not – quite – middleclass British suburbia. I like to think he nicely embodied the spirit of his country: the dark Indian mirror and the ruthless Spanish gaiety.

That bird had *cojones*. He became the best feathered companion anyone could hope for. Years later (and by then a gorgeous green, red and blue creature) he flew through the screen door and disappeared into a New Jersey snowstorm. A final cheerful squawk and he was off on what I have come to accept must have been Harry's journey to the Great Rainforest in the Sky.

Harry never said anything except 'Ari' and thereby revealed his name. He preferred to walk rather than fly although he always had fully operational wings: no clipping for Harry. He never lived in a cage, never had his foot tied again. He loved the instant monsoon of a warm shower and would sneak into a bathroom the moment he heard water ('My God! There's a *creature* in here!') to stand with sodden wings outstretched, eyes closed with bliss.

Harry the Fearless who would always attack dogs *on the ground*. Harry the Bird of Action flew on ahead into louche New Orleans bars to check them out for food, and liked nothing better than making off with a fried chicken wing. Harry the Alarm Clock's chosen method of waking up a person was to take one of their little toes in his secateur beak and squeeze ever so gently.

Harry the Flying Toothpick, always clamouring to stick his head in your mouth after meals to search around for this and that between the old molars.

Harry would nonchalantly notch an earlobe or puncture a beer can with his amazing beak. He would bite anyone (except me) rash enough to pet him and while they were staunching blood and wondering if it might be worth suing me, he'd as likely fly off with their best pen to crack it like a nut. He was a champion introducer, 'Gee, that bird's real neat. Will it say Lurleen? That's my name, and this is my friend Lola-May...') and he never, ever, shat on his friends.

As the large cook at Buster's Place on Bourbon Street said when she rushed out of her kitchen too late to stop Harry winging off with some New Orleans style barbecued spare-rib, 'Yes Sir! That bird something else!'

*

Planet Health Warning: of course, all this happened when I and the whole world were younger and foolisher. We now know that the wild animal trade is synonymous with distress and death throughout the world. Abducting animals from the wild for money is now unacceptable to us all (isn't it?). We now know better than to encourage it (don't we?). When I gave the poor old Mayan woman the dollar and took Harry off on foreign adventures I was probably helping to push him and his kind (the orange-winged Amazons) towards extinction. Guilty. I would be sad to have missed the time I had with my green friend, but a world without Harrys lurking in it somewhere would be impoverished indeed.

Samba-ing Along
with the Flow

BAHIA 1991

'We are very beautiful,' say the girls and the boys on the beaches. 'Watch me,' says the one-legged man as he chops open a coconut at his roadside stall. 'I'm irresistible,' says the traffic cop from behind his shades. 'I am the Madonna of the Sea,' says the old mammy who sells fried snacks on the corner. 'Me, me, me, me,' cry children as they beg with delicate, knowing gestures. Bahia is big, bold, black and beautiful. It loves itself. And it's got an appreciative eye on you too. You might as well samba along with the flow. And you might never be the same again.

Olodum, the most famous of the many Salvador drumming groups, practise in a yard off one of the alleyways near Pelhourinho Square, which is not an area highly recommended for a lone tourist to visit at night. If you go, an expat friend insisted, you must have *carranca* protection. A *carranca* (pronounced 'kahanka') is the grotesque carved wooden figure that wards off mishaps and evil spirits for São Francisco River boats. My *carranca* had a smile as big as Brazil and shoulders to match.

Carranca, whose real name is Cosme, is the boss and protector of a gang of car-minders at Terreiro de Jesus. Of him it's said, 'manda chuva': he can make it rain. Barely out of his teens, he's an old hand, a pillar of Street Establishment. With him along, about the worst thing that could happen to me (and it did) was getting an espadrille-full of something extremely fishy. We threaded our way through revellers gathered around a *trio elétrico* on a flat-bed truck. Cane spirit and beer circulated in the semi dark flagged alleyway. We headed for the Bar Banzo and Olodum.

Twenty-five drummers step back and forth in formation in an open yard jammed with fans samba-ing and passing bottles of beer overhead: the sound is like the falling of giant rocks. A torrential rhythm shakes your viscera and your plastic beer cup. From a balcony, singers join in, and favourite carnival numbers are echoed by the kids dancing below. As on the beaches, where congregations of boys and girls (in Brazil, the young vastly outnumber the old) strut their stuff in the kind of swim-wear they call 'dental floss'; the effect here is of decorous sexuality, un-innocent naiveté.

I'm captured by an undulant crowd of tropical youth, by unfamiliar perfumes and a spine-massaging drum beat. I am enjoying having my feet trodden on by beautiful girls. Salvador's drummers are hard-working hustlers by day who probably would be surprised to learn they are keeping up old African traditions. Slavery was not abolished here until 1888. Bahia, which imported slaves from West Africa for more than 400 years, is today easily the blackest part of South America. Yoruba words are still in everyday use. Pantheistic African Candomblé and Portuguese Catholicism have mingled like blood. In a typical family restaurant, a Sacred Heart of Jesus shares the wall-niche with flowers and other offerings to Xango the god of fire. At the big religious festivals, no one seems sure any more whether The Virgin or Yemanjá, the Yoruba sea goddess, is being venerated.

Even official figures admit that Salvador has about half a million homeless, destitute children. It is known that in 1990 at least 100 of these were murdered by vigilante death squads in the pay of local business interests. Against this chilling background, a certain amount of street wariness is called for, but I've encountered more menace on a provincial British Friday night. Our concept of recreational anti-social behaviour hasn't yet arrived in Brazil. Street kids here seem to consider the idea of violence without a sound motive – love or money – positively daft. Pinch-faced parents living in the notorious tar-paper *favelas* on the edges of the city, will carry water for miles so that their children can catch the school bus in clean clothes.

Marco's Paradise is 70-odd kilometres north from Salvador along the 'Coconut Highway'. After the road runs out of black-top, you have to negotiate ever bigger pot-holes on a dirt road until you come eventually to Praia do Forte, the earliest (1552) cattle ranch in the Americas. It's also the place where slash-and-burn farming started. Conquistador cattleman Garcia D'Avila's legacy is (along with a ruined fort and some responsibility for our ragged ozone layer) a private nature reserve that includes a large swamp *Pantanal*, home to more than 160 species of bird, and sandy forest *restinga* much favoured by bromeliads, cacti, orchids and cashews. There are 14 kilometres of coco-fringed turtle-inhabited Atlantic coast.

Struggling thigh-deep in warm swamp, I'd lost sight of young Marco, my guide and self-proclaimed Eco-Policeman. He'd got me into a steaming mangrove mess, far from the lost world of iced beer and air-conditioning at the hotel bar. Why had we abandoned the canoes? Was this some sort of swamp therapy? All around in the dappled sunlight under the mangroves were flowering lilies, exotic birds and rare orchids. Thoughts of bloodsuckers, electric eels, and even athlete's foot crept, stealthy as alligators, into my mind. It had cost me hours of prayerful concentration to master (i.e. stay afloat in) the little one-man plastic kayak, and just when I was beginning to relax and take in a few swamp impressions, Marco ran his canoe into a clump of vegetation, jumped down into three feet of brown water and said 'Now we must walking.' 'What, me?' I whinged.

'Don't, whatever you do, get into any South American rivers,' the doctor had said before I left England. 'Alligators and snakes are OK, really – it's the snails you have to worry about. Some of them carry bilharzia, a parasitic worm that gets in your blood and in your bladder.' I was reminded of these words when Marco had pointed out the big, black predatory birds that hovered all over the swamp. 'They are eating only *caracol* here,' he'd said. In other words, these were *snail kites*!

I caught up with Marco standing barefoot in the mud and staring up into the canopy with a strange look on his face. I was about to tell him about bladder attacks by the bilharzia worms, when he said, 'Shhh! Listen!' I couldn't hear anything at all. Just the usual bird noises, leaves moving overhead, the odd plop of something or other in the water. 'It is the sound of Paradiso,' murmured Marco. Twenty-one-year-old Marco ('I am autodidact eco-policemens') and his mate Jorge the Famous Surfer, hang out at a shed on the hotel beach, looking after boat hire, water skis, diving equipment and Mother Nature.

'This is Baby Piú,' said Jorge, introducing me to a tiny parrot they had confiscated from local peasant lads. 'When his wing feathers grow back he will be free again.' Little Piú packs the sort of nip that makes you wonder what a Big Piú bite might be like.

On his afternoon off, Marco was going to show me his nature beat, the *Pantanal*. He probably assumed, from some harmless exaggerations I might have made, that I was another Hiawatha. There was an electric-powered boat, he said, but for really getting *mano a mano* with swamp life, canoes were the thing. We would look for *jacaré*: alligators.

Slim, vegetarian, abstemious Marco led me with easy strokes into the hyacinth and lily-pad covered swamp. I was sweating and one leg had gone dead. The boat felt like a tight shoe. This was not shaping up to be one of those nice once-around-the-mangroves-and-back-in-time-for-tea-sort of expeditions.

In the bright heat of the *restinga* forest, where we emerged after our wade in the *Pantanal,* the sand was crowded with bromeliads and cacti. Orchids flourished in the clefts of short, tough trees. I noticed that the rotten ones had a most beguiling smell. Another delicious scent trailed from the indigo blossoms of cashew bushes. A sinister idea uncoiled itself: 'Marco,' I demanded, 'is *this* where you released all those snakes?' Marco – boy ecology-commando or veggie wimp nut-case, depending on how you stand on global greenery – had recently 'liberated' the entire snake collection from Salvador Zoo, constrictors, vipers and all. Exactly how he managed to get himself in and the snakes out he prefers to leave unexplained. Sacksful of snakes were smuggled back to his 'paradiso'. Police kept a baffled vigil at the city's hospitals for days expecting a snake-bitten burglar to turn up. 'It was just a Christmas present for the animals,' says Marco.

I was trying to stay as close to Marco as was consistent with making reasonable progress. As a tropical sunset began over the darkening forest, I wanted snakes to get the message: 'Don't bite me – I'm with him'. We found our canoes again, having waded through shimmying fire-flies to a frogs' chorus. Marco showed me alligators' eyes in the torch beam as the shy creatures took to the water in our wake. Very large bats jinked overhead.

I was beginning to feel just a touch pleased with myself: future dinner anecdotes had been piling up, and now that the canoe was pointed homewards my chances of surviving to tell looked quite good. Then, snug and smug in my little yellow boat, in the middle of a moonlit lagoon, I heard Marco say, 'This is trouble. It is bad mens.' Nonchalantly, Marco hauled a long net out of the water and stuffed it all into his canoe. That net, and the styrofoam floats that loomed faintly all around us in the mangroves, belonged to *jacaré* poachers. They'd laid 36 traps – large hooks baited with lumps of fish – only a couple or so hours before. In the moonlight, I helped Marco gather up the equipment as quickly as possible. I was not at all anxious to meet up with any of these bad mens. To get back to the hotel grounds, we had to carry our laden canoes past a police post. My suggestion that we should report the poachers earned a pitying shake of the head from Marco. Looking through the window into a bright interior where cops lounged with their guns and do-not-disturb reflecto-specs, I could see what he meant. These were not the sort of police you report things to. Brazilian back-country police – like legendarily beautiful women – just *are*.

Back at the shack on the beach, Marco showed me his large collection of confiscated *jacaré* hooks, now rusting in the salt air. We burned the net. Jorge opened a coconut. He mentioned that the local villagers had a new nickname for Marco: they called him Chico Mendes, after the Amazonian activist recently murdered for opposing rain-forest exploitation.

I didn't think I would sleep at all well if the local machete-toting hombres had started calling me Chico Mendes. Especially if they thought I was getting between them and illegal alligator skins worth more than two US dollars a square centimetre. Jorge and Marco found this idea highly amusing.

A Passionfruit as Big as the Ritz

BALI 1991

It must have rained like this in Eden. Through the blancmange of the windscreen, I can make out a roadside hoarding with a picture of a gigantic toothbrush. We are hemmed in by unmoving, steaming traffic. Italian-Swiss Maria, whose eight-year love affair with Bali might be going through a rough patch, turns off the engine and unconcernedly wields a mascara stick in the driving mirror. 'Rush-hour in paradise is always hell,' she mutters.

Hollywood used to be big on Bali. King Kong (if the charred maps featured at the start of so many jungle flicks were anything to go by) hailed from these dank, exotic regions. The location had a lot in common, I now realise, with the front rows of our local cinema from which my mates and I would yell boyish encouragement to cannibals or giant squid as they pursued Dorothy Lamour. She would be on *The Road to Bali* with Bob Hope and Bing Crosby. And we approved of Bali – it had big fruit, no school, and King Kong was our kind of ape.

That's why it comes as a bit of a surprise, shortly after landing at Denpasar Airport, to find myself stuck here in a traffic jam in a downpour, checking out the roadside ads and listening to gloomy stock market prices on the car radio. Like Maria's four-wheel-drive tonight, Indonesia, the multi-ethnic archipelago consisting of 13,677 equatorial islands with the world's fourth largest population, is sort of stuck. After being unbelievably up, the economy is now unbelievably down. The last time I was here, Indonesia was tigerishly clawing its way up. It had gone from being on a par with Bangladesh to being one of the World Bank's highest-performing pets. Where it is now, no one seems to know.

'Big volcano,' says Maria absently. She could be talking about Indonesia's economic, cultural and population pressures or my spluttering Surabaya clove cigarette. She could be referring to Mount Agung, which is hanging over the crowded motorway and King Kong's toothbrush like a stupendous watercolour.

But no matter how bad things get in Indonesia as a whole, Bali will always have its pre-eminent tourism niche. Sales coordinator Nyoman Kastawa tells me, over dinner at the plush Sanur Beach Hotel, how this small island, 90 miles long by 50 miles wide, still gets the lion's share of Indonesia's five million yearly visitors.

Concentrating on tourism figures is difficult when you're being hypnotised by the hotel's after-dinner entertainment. Gamelan is trance-inducing: a fizz of gongs, an orchestral tick-tocking of buffalo horn hammers on bronze. And while this is going forward, *Legong* dancers, perspiring under their heavy make-up and brocaded silks, are curling their toes as if they were creeping on cold lino. Little cymbals are exploding in the midst of low, almost subliminal chimes.

Our four dancers fan their back-curving fingers and work us over with their eyes. It's a cliché tourist event but it's also ravishing. And Noël Coward got it all wrong when he said, 'there is *far* too much music on Bali, and though as a place it's entrancing, there's also a *thought* too much dancing.'

Absorbed by gong harmonics and the slow, hieratic gestures of the dancers, I hear (as from another world) Mr Kastawa explaining, 'we used to just have bikes. Now we're one hundred per-cent four-wheel drive. But there's a little problem right now about keeping up the payments.' 'I dedicate this to the memory of the 100,000 rickshaws that have been banished from the streets of Jakarta,' announces Wahyoe the artist when I drop in at his studio behind the gift shops of Kuta Beach.

He jabs another gobbet of paint onto a collage occupying an entire wall. Wahyoe, who was born in Java nearly 50 years ago, satirises some of his country's recent socio-economic history thus: 'We struck oil. We got cheap petrol. National pride demanded we outlaw that colonial abomination the rickshaw.'

An Australian woman perches on a cushion in the doorway and shows a semi-anthropological interest in Wahyoe's traditional torso and arm tattoos. He adjusts one of the old bike wheels incorporated into his latest *oeuvre* and, with a hitch to his sarong and the ghost of a conspiratorial wink in my direction, pads over to the big fridge for more beer.

It has been Bali's fate to appeal to outsiders' often-prurient ideas about what constitutes an earthly paradise. Within half a dozen years of the bloody annexation of this uniquely Hindu island into the Dutch East Indies, when thousands of Bali's aristocracy, including old people, mothers and children, performed *puputan*, the ritual suicide march, the first tourist brochures of 1914 were featuring bare-breasted village woman and going on about 'this unforgettable Garden of Eden.' By 1930, Bali was up to 100 or so tourists a month and was becoming renowned for paintings, carvings and fabrics, and (those nubile brochure-girls notwithstanding) known also for perceived easy-going sexual attitudes among its young unmarried men. These days, according to Maria, the boys of Bali are a main attraction for Japanese women tourists.

Ant and Garth from Melbourne, on the other hand, tend to inspire passion in the breasts of Kuta Beach bar waiters. This is because Ant and Garth can sit at a table all night without buying a drink. I catch up with these leggy and laconic surfers one night at the Sari Club along Kuta's frantic Legan Street. Under the exasperated eyes of the waiters, they sprawl (these boys could sprawl for Australia) never far from their gallon plastic containers of supermarket orange-juice. They and all the other Aussie kids are here to drink their own OJ, talk surf and catch the pheromones.

'Kuta's a tradition… our dads came here,' says Ant. 'And me Mum did when she was a hippy,' adds Garth. We all watch the suntanned white girls dancing. I pay for a beer and my waiter disappears into the throng. Ant predicts (correctly it turns out), 'You'll never see yer change, mate.'

Well, you lose some and you win some. An unprepossessing eatery smack bang in the heart of raving Kuta turns out to be a frangipani-scented haven providing satay chicken, local fish, prawns, vegetables and rice, with a couple of beers, for less than a fiver.

The gift shop next door to my restaurant has its cheapo stock laid out on an old silk sarong, batik, of flowers and cockerels. The thing is stained, has some holes, and the lovely indigo swirls have gone black. Still, it's very Dorothy Lamour. 'Old Bali,' explains the shopkeeper wearily, getting ready to close up for the night. It isn't really for sale; she names a daft price to put me off.

She is as surprised as I am when I immediately hand over 25 crisp new American dollars. I like to think that the bold spirit of King Kong made me do it. 'You should have eaten at one of the stalls beside the motorway,' Maria tells me next day as we drive into the interior. 'You can get meat-balls, noodles, fried rice, the works, for about 40 pence.'

The narrow road takes us through villages and a rising landscape of flooded rice terraces where peasant grannies in conical hats stoop in the mud. With clouds reflected all around, it's as if we are flying through the warm, wet middle of the sky.

We arrive in Ubud at least 20 years too late. This hilly, lush region, an hour or so's drive from Denpassar was, in the days of the Rajas, famous for its devotional carvings. Now, Ubud supplies knick-knackery for the mantelpieces of the world. The coterie of expat western aesthetes who made Ubud the *in* place during the 1930s (attracting, among others, Charlie Chaplin, Noël Coward and Barbara Hutton) inadvertently started what became a major industry.

'For those, you need a very strong mantelpiece,' says Maria drily as I hop out of the car to photograph a workshop full of nearly life-sized horses.

Each community in the area has perfected its own particular carved wood product: the village of Mas devotes itself to cats, at Tengallang it's all fruit and flowers (the extraordinarily realistic banana trees come in six sizes) and in Tengkulak it's birds.

In a Tengkulak backyard, dogs snooze under baulks of timber in the rain, and women with infants at their breasts are busy sandpapering hundreds of seagulls. Under an awning, a young man studies a well-thumbed German bird book. Ketut Sudarta is finding out where exactly to place the black patches on *Larus argentatus*, a bird he's never likely to see in the flesh. Ketut and his family are making 1,300 of these, to them exotic, herring gulls for a Düsseldorf gift shop.

Souvenir emporiums line the roads in and out of Ubud for miles: dazzling painted fish by the ocean-load, eerie armies of masks and ever-receding plantations of wooden banana trees. Credit cards are welcomed. Madé, a carver friend of Maria's, admits that he is now worried that supplies of hardwood are running out. The price of teak, mahogany, jacaranda, jackfruit and hibiscus, escalates. Large timbers such as are needed for the horses of Peliatan, he says, can now be found only in remote parts of Java and Sumatra. 'But all things must come from the gods,' he says matter-of-factly, lighting a stick of incense at the little offering-place near the workshop door.

The gods live on Mount Agung. An hour or so's drive eastwards and upwards from Ubud through exquisite cloudlands of rice brings us to the sacred volcano of Agung and to Pura Besakih, the Great Mother Temple which crouches over its brood of 21 smaller temples.

Worshippers and priests in bright silks sit cross legged under pagodas in a misty, lava-grey landscape. The defiant sound of crowing drifts up the valley, probably issuing from the pampered fighting birds of Tenganan a few miles to the south east. There, whole families still sometimes spend years making enough ikat cloth for a single sarong, pre-dyeing every warp and weft thread before starting the weave.

Little fruit stalls line the walk down from Besakih to the road, so I buy a perfume-exuding yellow globe resembling a dinosaur egg. When the leathery skin is bitten through, I and several other tourists are sprayed with a kind of heavenly frog-spawn. It's a passionfruit as big as the Ritz and it tastes like sweet and sour paradise.

Cruel Cargo

Beautiful South American birds, especially macaws, parrots, hornbills and toucans, are still making illegal fortunes for wildlife merchants despite tough new international agreements to suppress the trade. Exotic birds are often sold through the notorious wildlife markets of the Far East, finding avid buyers from Europe and the United States. Birds that are trapped by forest Indians and sold to local dealers for a few pence, change hands later for hundreds of pounds. Wildlife agencies reckon that for every wild bird sold, at least ten die along the way as they are smuggled or 'laundered' with false documents to appear as legitimate captive-bred imports. This is the story of one such cargo:

Nobody knows how many of the estimated, 2,000 wild tropical birds that comprised the *Connie Marie's* last cargo, died on their way from the South American mainland to Grenada, the most southerly of the Windward Islands. Rare toucans and hornbills, macaws and parrots were crammed into cages in the stifling dark below the scruffy little coaster's decks. Many birds died and were simply dumped overboard as the boat made her way from South America via Trinidad. Some were just left to putrefy in the bottom of crowded, filthy cages.

When the *Connie Marie*, which might not be her real name (there are persistent rumours she changed from *Shirene* during an emergency repair stop in Trinidad) sailed into St George's tourist attraction harbour, there was yet more suffering in store for its unfortunate, living cargo. They were transferred to a nearly windowless concrete shed in the grounds of the island's derelict and empty zoo. Twenty years before, the building had been used as a government quarantine station; now, iron sheets were nailed over the windows and the birds were locked away in the dark, still in their tiny wire and wood cages.

Inadequate water and food, heat and overcrowding, were to kill many more in the weeks ahead. Rumours began to circulate. Concerned members of the Grenada Society for the Prevention of Cruelty to Animals were threatened with violence by 'minders' with Guyana accents when they tried to investigate the building. They managed, eventually, to get near enough to peer through cracks.

'That shed was a vision of Hell – a Dachau Concentration Camp for animals,' said John Albanie, a Briton resident in Grenada and President of the GSPCA.

'The noise was awful, and there was the real stink of death in there. Animals in small boxes were piled up all over the floor. Many were very sick. Most had running eyes and damaged wings. There were a lot of dead and pecked birds. Animals in the throes of death lay on their backs in faeces. We managed to sneak in there when a guard wasn't looking and saw hundreds of birds crammed into tiny cages. One box, only about a metre long, had 26 toucans in it.'

Enraged members daubed the words 'Mad House' on the building...and they started putting pressure on the Grenada government to save the birds. Embarrassed ministers clearly felt compromised by the fact that government permits had been granted to one Jagdeshwar Lall Sadhu (a.k.a. Jagdeshwar Lall) citizen of Guyana much sought-after by US wildlife authorities concerning charges of illegal importation into Florida of rare birds, to trade in birds and even set up a working 'zoo' on the island. After some legal skirmishes in which Sadhu claimed compensation of nearly one million dollars, the Grenada government seized the bird collection and banned Sadhu and his employees from the site. Sadhu promptly disappeared and the GSPCA were asked to take charge while the birds' fate was decided.

Evidence is still coming to light of Sadhu's frantic efforts to dispose of birds as he realised that the Grenada government was going to act against him. At least three shipments of the birds were air-freighted out of Grenada, the last one, to Singapore, less than a month before the 'zoo' was closed down. Finally, he even offered the birds for sale to the general public, inviting people to come along and take their pick and pay cash on the nail.

One of his customers was Wendy Cooper, who runs a small hotel and wildlife sanctuary on the nearby island of Carriacou: 'It was hellish. Sick and dying and stressed birds everywhere. We went along posing as prospective customers so that we could collect evidence about this ghastly operation, and in fact we actually purchased a green-winged and a blue and gold macaw and a large Amazon parrot in order to save their lives.

'The macaws were in some sort of shock and their wings were badly damaged. The parrot was blind. We just paid Sadhu what he asked, which was a lot. He even had the nerve to phone some days afterwards offering me commissions if I could persuade some of my friends to buy more!'

By the time GSPCA volunteers moved in, there were only 256 birds left, many of which were dangerously stressed and damaged. The wings of some macaws and parrots had been permanently damaged by brutal clipping. There were many eye infections.

'Looking after wild birds properly calls for lots of skills and lots of money – we were short on both counts,' admits John Albanie. Local businesses donated cracked corn, rice, fruit etc., and volunteers moved the birds into open-air cages and began a round-the-clock care programme. Prime Minister Nicholas Brathwaite topped up the government allocation from his own pocket. 'At last, we were doing something for the birds,' said John when he showed me round the dark and smelly but now empty 'Mad House', which still had a few British Airways freight boxes piled on the floor.

'We and the Grenada government soon realised we'd been left with a massive problem: where were the birds going to live? Looking after them as a public collection would cost more than Grenada could afford; returning them to the wild would cost even more, assuming it were possible. Vets told us that the birds posed a considerable health risk to the island.'

The pathetic, beautiful victims of Mr Sadhu's business venture came close to being humanely destroyed. At last, a permanent home was found for them with the CITES-approved World Bird Sanctuary in Missouri. All the birds have now been flown to the United States. WBS specialises in breeding from wild birds and have promised Grenada help in setting up any future public bird collection.

Meanwhile, back in St George's harbour, a man rows out to the *Connie Marie*. Now an empty hulk, looking the very picture of a disreputable rust-bucket at the end of a chequered life in the South American coastal trade, she shifts forlornly on the tide. She has been run aground to prevent her sinking. A red and blue parrot's feather is stuck to some tar on the deck. In the midday sun, everything is too hot to touch. Flaking paint reveals that there could be something in the name-change rumour. The smell of death still wafts up from below deck. The man in the dinghy is very friendly. He is not Jagdeshwar Lall Sadhu. 'That man sell to me this boat. Cheap!' he tells me, grinning. Does he know where I might find Mr S.?

'That Sadhu, Sir...he gone!'

Raiders of the Lost Ouzo

GREECE 1992

Down among the sea-cucumbers was a bottle. It glinted as I looked down through my diving mask and flippered my way ashore. And that's how I came to be walking backwards up a beach on a north Aegean island, clutching a bottle of Ouzo.

This was Thassos, and the yacht I'd arrived in sat opulently at anchor, far out in the bay. I was still admiring it through the watery glass of my mask when a voice in my ear said 'Thanks, Pal, ye've found wor bottle for us!'

Blinkered, and going heels first (the easiest way to walk in flippers) I had emerged from the waves into the midst of a large party of young package tourers, all from Newcastle. They were having a game of beach cricket, with a crate of empty bottles for stumps. Alarmingly pink boys in Union Jack shorts chanted their gratitude. The ball was lost, temporarily, in some thorny rocks. A girl outfielder seemed to be having hysterics in the surf.

I learned that the Ouzo had fallen overboard when these lads and lasses were coming ashore in their tour company's motor boat. They were on a 'mystery' outing and had been marooned they knew not where. They had been dumped, together with a very large supply of alcohol and some fizzy drinks, on this remote beach, and the boat had disappeared after promises from the skipper that he'd return in time to get everyone back to their hotels for dinner and the disco. Now, the party had started to flag, someone had hit the ball into a nearby wilderness, and the booze was getting low. Chaos, one suspected, was creeping in. Everyone agreed that my arrival with the lost Ouzo couldn't have come at a better moment.

Back on the ship, the captain's wife, Aliki, had scanned the cricketers through binoculars. muttering 'Oh, good shot!' and 'Go on, run for it!' With what seemed to me typical Greek generosity of spirit, she wasn't at all put out by the invasion of 'her' beach. The British captain and I, on the other hand, thought it was a bit much.

The truth was, we – the captain and I – had been thinking of the place as 'ours' since we had set out to find it. After all (we reasoned) wasn't the bay part of Aliki's birthright? The little crescent with its surrounding hills covered in wild olives and pine trees and arbutus, had been where she, as a child, had sailed every year for family picnics. There, she chased butterflies and lizards, threw pebbles at the sea, and squabbled and larked with her sister and brothers and cousins. Comprehensive Greek family meals had gone on for whole summer days. The nearest road was miles away inland. Didn't all this give our party some sort of proprietorial rights? Well, the sun was shining impartially on us all and Aliki was obviously enjoying everything too much to have any patience with our suburban territoriality.

Sailing south from Kavala, on the northern mainland, we had thought it would be exciting to reunite Aliki with the place, and to show it to Thalia and Kathleen, the two small daughters. Our sea chart had a name for the area, Agios Georgios, and it seemed to know something the ordinary land map, which showed no features, didn't, for there must have been a settlement there. Aliki thought she remembered finding old apple trees on the slopes. Finding the magical picnic ground of her childhood, we thought, would make a good excuse for an Odyssey.

Actually, we'd had quite a trip, even sailing through some
Atlantic-style switchbacks as we explored our way around Thassos
and encountered the late summer *meltemi*. It made us think how
hazardous this wind must have been for the ships of ancient times.
Old folk on the islands say the *meltemi* can make people stone mad
and, at the very least, is a provoker of bad dreams. All I can attest
is that the chop that follows after the *meltemi* is a sure bringer of
sea-sickness. Thassos is famous for honey and marble, and once
dominated the Macedonian coast as a centre of gold-mining. There
are a lot of classical features still, including an amphitheatre and
a sanctuary to Pan. The captain and I swam ashore at an ancient
quarry, carrying our boots around our necks, intent on prospecting
the streambeds coming down from Mount lpsarion. We found a
sheep bell (around the neck of a long-dead ewe) and took it along
for a new life as a ship's bell. We got lost on mountain slopes covered
in bee-hives, drank from springs and ate the (rather tasteless)
arbutus berries. We stumbled into the old village of Theologos
where we were given some *karydaki* – a dark, treacly mixture of
unripe walnuts preserved in honey. We found pyrites and some
curious, black, metallic dust, a dung-beetle or two, but no sign of
the legendary gold.

The old marble quarryings, on the south-east coast, were
remarkable. A whole promontory carved out, often right down to
sea-level, so that it had become possible to walk off the edge of a
smooth, white plateau into 80 metres of water. Curious erosion had
created hundreds of bath-shaped depressions, very restful and
surreal places to loll. At a small anchorage on one side of the quarry,
an old woman in black was gathering sea-snails, and Aliki explained
to Thalia and Kathleen (I was agog, too) about octopuses' gardens.
They are not figments of the Beatles' imaginations. We all dived
down about eight feet with the mask to see a garden she had found.
There, as promised, was a rock surrounded by sand and on one side
of the rock was a small semi-circle of stones and shell-fragments –
the garden of an octopus. I thrust my face close to the garden and

saw, in a gap, another eye looking back. I can report that an octopus has a very *sensible* eye.

Aliki's magic bay was on the north, the lusher, wetter side of the island, facing slightly west. She had recognised it immediately from far at sea. The party of young Geordies who swam out to *Calyx* were as much impressed by being offered real British tea and biscuits as by the fact that *Calyx* had taken the captain seven years to build in a Cambridgeshire barn. They were fed up with some of their tour organisers: 'They handle us with tongs, like, as if we were all football hooligans,' said beautiful, chain-smoking Marilyn.

Sure enough, a surly boatman came in the evening to scoop them up, 'Let's go! Let's go! Let's go!' he yelled, letting out a deafening hooter blast and revving the engine. We stood on our deck and waved goodbye, and suddenly all was quiet. Then we rowed over to the beach to watch the stars come out.

Serranía de Ronda

SPAIN 1992

Silvia came through the door and leaned her rucksack against the bar. She hitched up torn shorts and stretched her bare arms over her head, bent over and touched her toes a couple of times – sun-bleached hair falling over sea-green eyes – and then plonked down onto a stool amongst the watching old farmers at the bar. 'So! I think I find you in such a pub,' she told me accusingly over her shoulder.

Poncia, in Lorca's *The House of Bernarda Alba*, bemoans married men's interests descending through three stages: Bed to Table to Tavern. But in the Bar Nuevo in the Andalusian mountain village of Alpandeire, the trend was going the opposite way. The farmers, most of whom should have been home hours before, were suddenly pulling in their stomachs, calling out for more wine and tapas, and raising 80-cigarettes-a-day baritone shouts. I and my notebook, till then subjects of some mild interest, were left alone to study a collection of old government notices on the wall.

Did you know that the southern end of the Iberian Peninsula is a particularly favourite stopping-off point for large numbers of the world's birds of passage? Or that you shouldn't trap insectivorous birds such as *Saxicola torquatus* and *Anthus pratensis* because they can each consume two and a half kilos of insects a year?

I was going to ask Silvia if she had noticed any of these birds on our hard walk out of the last valley, but she was busy entrapping a significant part of the Stage Three population of the village, a group who, I couldn't help noticing, were themselves not bad consumers. Wine, wine and more wine, together with plates of raw ham and olives, disappeared into a noisy circle at the bar.

In the centre perched Silvia, sweetly explaining in her city Spanish that were it not for her present duties as translatrix, guide and pointer-out of the straight and narrow to 'El periodista Inglés' (I looked apologetic but no one noticed) this was just the sort of village, the very *corazón* of Andalusia where she would like to stay for a while and really get to know the people...because she was getting a bit tired of Malaga...which had become just like any other big city...and now that she was older (Silvia would be 23 in a month's time) she was feeling it was almost time to get a bit closer to Beautiful Nature. There followed a deep, sea-lion murmuring of approval, regret, understanding, appreciation – calls for more wine.

Miguel, the landlord, brought out a plastic container of his famous home-made wine, which managed to be at once cloudy, sweet and sour. It could, I decided after a while, grow on a person. Silvia waved gaily and got one of the farmers to bring me a plate of raw, wind-dried ham. It had the faintly corrupt perfume of the real Fata Negra from the mountains. 'I looking after you!' she shouted.

Silvia first popped into my life as a part-time barmaid at the Pike and Eel in Cambridge. Her parents must have assumed she was attending one of the more usual language schools. She liked to interrupt my crossword routine with hair-raising details of her love life.

Once, when I made dinner for Silvia and a girl-friend of hers, they giggled and chain-smoked and got hysterical about boys all through the meal, casually wolfing down a little number composed of octopus, pine nuts, olives and shallots cooked in wine, under the impression (I later found out) that it was some kind of spaghetti.

After Silvia went back to family and fiancé in Spain, I got occasional cards and letters in half-Spanish mynah bird English: I was not to forget to tell my great friend whenever I was to going Malaga. She met me at the airport. 'You fat,' she said gravely.

'I'm going for a walk in the Serranía de Ronda,' I told her. On the train into town, Silvia explained that she had just lost her *novio* to one of Malaga's barmier fundamentalist sects. He now had the gift of tongues and a wife. 'So I walking too. You will not drink beer and eat too much and you will be being thin. And I will not smoking cigarettes so I will become very beautiful.' 'It's a deal.'

The Malaga coastline, representing as it does one of the more porous margins of Europe, has a relishable loucheness. On the train inland to Ronda – a perfect HQ from which to explore the Serranía – I had written in my notebook: 'Sects, Drugs and Flamenco.' I was quite pleased with that. It earned a pitying shake of the head from Silvia as she went out to the corridor for a fag.

Ronda has such good, old-fashioned pubs (some pretty nifty old buildings, too, including one of Spain's oldest bullrings) that I was tempted to extend my research programme here. The place had been a favourite haunt of Rilke and Hemingway, I explained, but Silvia was having none of that. She couldn't say 'Rilke' (whoever that was) and didn't approve of Hemingway. We shouldered our rucksacks and headed off beyond the bullfight big hills. White-washed austere villages among cherry-orchards, vines, walnuts and chestnuts. Higher up are cork oaks and umbrella pines and the rare Spanish silver fir. Roadside springs of icy, delicious water, gave me welcome excuses to stop and have a closer look at rockroses, hollyhocks, foxgloves and dianthus. 'Why you always ask what they called?' said Silvia, who had a townie's tendency to gather bouquets along the way. To Silvia, flowers were simply flowers, and clearly I was not appreciating them properly.

Even the smallest village will have its church, taverna and little general store around a plaza. The plazas, always deserted except for one sleeping dog, were good places to rest and enjoy penknife feasts of cheese and tomatoes and the excellent local charcuterie. Silvia (her big knife, I noticed warily, was sharp enough to shave with) would carve chorizos and slabs of *carne de membrillo* – a kind of stiff, astringent jelly made from quinces.

Roads in the Serranía, wide and solid on the tourist map, often turned out to be (I'm glad to say) dirt-tracks. Some river-valleys (I'm still glad to say) can't be crossed by car, although we often passed road-building gangs. It won't be long before tourers will be able to pass straight through this region in a few hours. We had to wade the River Genal and then heroically climb out of the valley on an endless white dust road to get to Júzcar as dusk came on. Collapsing under some brutal strip-lighting at the village's social centre, we learned that the village, like many in the area, had no official overnight facilities. After that climb, I boasted, I could easily sleep upside-down on a sharp rock. 'Ha! He's much too spoiled for that!' Silvia told the villagers crushingly, and went off to see the *alcalde* and arrange lodgings at the house of an old couple.

Under an animal feed calendar portraying The Stigmata, Maria, the landlady at the Bar Tropesén in the village of Faraján, creator of world-class egg, ham, chips and salad, watched with approval as I demolished her handiwork. Silvia was at the bar driving the local men crazy. Later, when I squeezed through to the bar for a glass of wine and the unrefusable tapas of Serrano ham, I remembered to ask her why she disapproved of Hemingway.

'He was fat!' she cried.

Maharaja of All He Purveys

RAJASTHAN 1993

'Outside these walls one is nobody,' admits Kesri Singh, sitting at
ease in his garden behind the high, cannonball-chipped walls of
Castle Mandawa, overlooking an oasis in the middle of Rajasthan.
A movement of his hand, and another drink instantly appears. The
servant backs away into the evening twilight. Kesri Singh's cigarette
describes an arc as he waves expansively at his guests. To them – in
accents ranging from Paris (France) to Paris (Texas) – he is simply
'the Maharaja'. He has rediscovered the pleasure and profit to be had
from playing the royal host – five centuries after his family line split
from that of the Maharajas of Jaipur, and just a few years since he
was pushing a pen in a bank.

Kesri Singh, grandson of the Thakur of Mandawa, was born at
the same time as Independence, and has never been nostalgic about
the legacies and foibles of India's cricketing conquistadores. Post-Raj
India brought hard times for many old aristocratic families like the
Singhs. Government stipends, established generations before by
the British, were cut off. Kesri went to work in a bank. When he was
home on leave one day his grandfather took him for a walk around
the fairytale battlements of Castle Mandawa and revealed that the

family was going broke. As a hardworking and punctilious clerk, Kesri didn't fancy the time-honoured Singh remedy for lack of cash: despoiling the local peasantry. Instead, he took the – for a Mandawa Singh – drastic course of going into business. 'When I turned the place into an hotel, I was not at all sure how this would go down in the family – or, for that matter with the servants… who had all been hanging around here for generations.

'After all, we had always been warriors and so on. My ancestors just went out there and took whatever they wanted. From an historical point of view, hotel keeping didn't seem to be our style.'

Castle Mandawa is now a place where the world and its suitcases can be found, 'It's right up my street,' says Kesri, who is still trying to establish exactly how many rooms and how many servants he has.

Despite that vagueness about servants and rooms, and in contrast to the unruly style of his forebears, he keeps a meticulous, clerkly eye on the business. He has large bookings well into the next two years. And the servants love the new regime, 'That one does tend to over-act a bit, doesn't he?' commented Kesri approvingly of one of his turbanned staff.

Some servants, I was assured, were selected purely for the ethnic luxuriance of their moustaches. There had even been cases of prize 'specimens' being lured away by rival hotels in Jaipur. The family's hereditary food-taster 'He's old; obviously nobody has tried to poison us for ages!' now precedes the bringing-in of dinner at Castle Mandawa. Lit by torches and accompanied by musicians, the procession goes at the pace dictated by the old man's amazing gyroscopic dancing. 'He says that although he is much too old to dance now, he can still do it so long as I keep giving him whisky,' said Kesri.

Castle Mandawa arises out of a flat, featureless landscape, Ely Cathedral style, girdled by a small town seeming to huddle for protection at its base. Mandawa, surrounded by a sand desert, was once a turbulent oasis on the camel caravan route between the Middle East and China, connecting the coast of Gujarat to Delhi, which was why Kesri's ancestors (family motto: The Brave Rule the World) built the Castle, installed impressive cannon and put a frieze of anti-elephant spikes all over their front door.

By accounts they were a pretty argumentative lot, these Mandawa Singhs, always quarrelling with their distant relatives, the kings of nearby Jaipur. The last feud was in the 1820s and is remembered as the Battle of the Cannons. The outcome was one-nil to Mandawa – according to Kesri the result of a single, inspired shot from the home side's inebriated master-gunner.

Today, the famous cannon rests in the heat and dust of one of the Castle's camel-yards, and in the gate-house a servant has the job of manufacturing, every hour, a version of Big Ben chimes. After a wobbly tape has been run through the tannoy system, hours are counted off by hand on a big brass gong. What would happen, I wondered, if the gate-house man (imperfectly awoken from his doze, say, in the middle of a hot Rajasthan day) were to strike the gong a wrong number of times? 'I would have him fired out of the cannon!' said the master of Mandawa.

When it comes to getting things done in rural India, being a near-enough Maharaja makes all the difference, and the skills of his office-wallah days have enabled Kesri to design and build a complete village-style annex, a mile or two out in the desert, in three months. That's the sort of time, normally, it would take a local government *babu* to finish scratching his ear and ask you what you wanted.

Kesri's desert village is for the Castle's more adventurous guests, who, having been jack-knifed aloft on the backs of vengeful and capricious camels, now have somewhere to head for through the dunes. Eagles, parrots and bee-eaters live there, among scant Khejri thorns.

Eagles hang all day on the air currents around the walls of Castle Mandawa. You can easily find yourself looking one in the eye as you pass on different sides of a turret window, and Kesri likes to tell the story of one of his guests having lunch stolen from under their knife and fork by a swooping bird.

To walk past the snoozing Westminster chimes man and through the elephant gates is to enter, suddenly, into timeless (the occasional transistor blare or multi-coloured blancmange of a TV notwithstanding) pestering India. The chai-shop in Mandawa turned out to be the meeting place of the disciples of a local holy man. I was shown postcards of a *sadhu* sitting in the lotus position and covered in what looked like red and yellow paint. This man, they said, was a famous devotional musician and played an instrument the name of which I couldn't quite catch at first, although it was familiar. Yamaha! And sure enough, a postcard showed the *sadhu*, cross-eyed and bedizened, posing at an electronic keyboard.

The official attraction of Mandawa is the frescoed houses – *havelis* – that surround the Castle and once housed the Shekhawati merchants who flourished there for about 100 years until the 1930s when the elaboration of the railways finally did away with the need for camel routes. Paintings cover the outsides and insides of the impressive houses of a monied merchant caste. When it came to business (I remembered being told by a Balliol-educated Indian) Jains were reckoned to be the bee's knees.

A chaste kiss between two young turn-of-the-century European visitors was thought so extraordinary that their flirtation can still be seen, larger than life on the side of a house. There is also a picture of an early flying machine and others showing the first, fateful loco-motives, as well as scenes of courtly Indian life amid flowers and animals.

Lohars, the original nomadic smiths from which stock our own gypsies are descended, still camp on the edge of town with their distinctive wagons and their air of louche outsiderdom. They work – even on traffic islands in the middle of Delhi thoroughfares – at primitive pit-forges. Their women are attractive and wear revealing bodices.

A boy with a rattle, a trick dagger and three bicycle bells took advantage of the annoying crowd that I had attracted, to put on his show. It was wonderful. He made a pretend stab at another urchin and the dagger sprouted a red paper flower which, for an instant, looked like blood.

'This poor boy; give him two rupees,' said the old man next to me. The child-magician demanded five. The man, after looking hard in my direction as if he was trying to recall some important message, suddenly said in a voice like Lucky's in *Waiting for Godot*; 'Greece is a large, hot country occupying the top right-hand corner of the map. The sun shines most of the year. The people are Christians and engage in agriculture...'

Fleeing the further demands of the magician and the rote-learned echo of that ancient school lesson, I backed into a shoe-shop and found myself half a step from a drop into an open sewer. Tuning out the shopman's spiel, I imagined the piquant scenario that could follow the descent of a litigiously-inclined New World guest like the New Jersey dentist I'd been talking to at breakfast...

I hurried back to the Castle. On the way, two matronly Scandinavian women were having their free, non-handbag clutching hands sweetly and very firmly held by tiny barefoot beggars. I beat them all to the welcoming spikes of the elephant gate.

'This boy used to work as a coolie down there in the village,' announced Kesri as I arrived sweatily at the top of the stone entrance stairs. He indicated a young man, decked out in a brand-new Castle uniform. The boy looked uneasy, but chuffed. 'I was telling him,' said Kesri Singh, 'Your grandfather was in charge of the Mandawa treasury, and here you are – that man's grandson! Grubbing in the earth. Come to the Castle and I'll give you a proper job.'

Castle Mandawa's Maharaja snapped his fingers. 'Now he will get us some tea. You're just in time.'

Surfing Away from Jesus

BAHIA 1993

Sunday morning in Bahia. Grey clouds loom in from the Atlantic and, from six floors up at the Sofitel Hotel, I can see palm trees on a deserted beach beyond golf links. I'm within earshot of the main runway of Salvador Airport. It's raining, warm, and on the TV in the corner a man in a psychedelic suit is trying to sell me Jesus.

I'm not buying. But a browse through the channels confirms there's no escape. A Florida evangelist with designer beard and Friar Tuck haircut totes a cross of telephone pole dimensions and demands money. What could be a tasteless stage hypnotism act, with supplicants having fits and being poleaxed by pats on the head is accompanied by requests for donations. The Suit, meanwhile, wheels out a smug-looking housewife who, he claims, gave her last few *cruzeiros* to Jesus – and then won a small fortune in a lottery. Giving money, we understand, will give us a hotline to the miraculous.

This wearying stuff, jamming Sunday TV and spilling out of football grounds and car-parks during the week, with its relentless Country and Western accompaniment, is getting on my paranoias. Two weeks in Brazil and I'm almost ready to believe in a white-trash, glow-in-the-dark, world-domination conspiracy. Definitely time to karate the 'off' button and go down to breakfast. I'm getting the plane to London in a few hours. I want to sniff the real Brazil just once more. I don't want to spend the last day of my trip being doorstepped in my own bed by Nazarene Promotions Inc. I need a walk on the beach... before I do something daft like sending off for a magnetic Dashboard Saviour.

Protestant fundamentalism is reckoned to be making headway – in what was always regarded as the world's largest nominally Roman Catholic country – at the rate of something like 600,000 converts a year, according to my previous night's conversation with poet-turned-journalist Guillhermo Esquival. That's what it says in my notebook anyway, jotted down after we'd conversed our way through several *caipirinhas*, the knockout national tipple of sugarcane spirit, limes, sugar and crushed ice. Senhor Esquival, I noted, finds the whole business depressing on aesthetic grounds. 'I'm much afraid one morning I wake up and find everybody wearing a gringo baseball-hat that says "Put your heart in Heaven or get your ass out".' He blamed television for everything.

Favela dwellers throw bare wires over overhead power cables to get electricity (the Church of Our Lord of Good Endings, Nosso Senhor do Bonfim, has a wall just for thank-offerings for deliverance from near electrocutions, and one evening we'd driven to an Armageddon-sized slum on the far edge of Salvador). Every stick-and-cardboard shack seemed to glow with bluish TV light. 'See, it's a Trojan horse. It can put Bible Belt God-salesmen right into the *favela*. Our governments tolerate them because they find *laissez-faire* anti-socialist doctrines – no matter how...what you call barmy? – reassuring. These guys are not talking Liberation Theology.' Over his *caipirinha* Senhor Esquivel mused: 'I worry about this baseball hat thing...'

There are plenty of baseball hats, as it happens, among the noisily dressed tourists being shepherded by immaculate porters in the hotel foyer. The wearers don't actually look like the cultural shock-troops of redneckism. They're mostly pear-shaped golfers.

I'm on my way, after the hotel's brilliant Anglo/Brazilian breakfast of eggs, bacon and toasted *mandioca* meal, to that palm-tree beach for (I hope) a final loiter in real, unsanctified Brazil.

As far as I can remember, I'll have to go out at the back and simply keep on going...beyond the proper walkways and gardens, beyond the far reaches of the golf-course. Beyond even the drain-diggers and golf-ball retrievers. After this point I start to feel a bit furtive. I'm alone on a tropical track beside an endless fence. I've lost sight of the hotel. I'm wondering if, to find my beach with the palm trees, I might have to climb over the fence.

An armed man in a watchtower nearly hidden among trees does a horrified double-take when he happens to glance down and spot me. *I'm in the wrong place!* He's supposed to be guarding the small metal door set in the fence, but not from people like me. Discommoding a guest would cost him his job. He freezes unhappily. I slip through the door, giving what I hope is a reassuring wave, into another world.

I'm in a ditch. A track leads me among rubbish-blown bushes until I'm standing under a bright, rainy sky beside a motorway. A barefooted old black man goes by pushing a wheelbarrow made out of the shell of a refrigerator. I can hear music. I walk across steamy concrete overgrown with purple trumpet vines towards my palm trees, which I have just glimpsed sticking out beyond some shacks. From the dark interior of a wooden hut comes the sound of voices passionately arguing. In a yard, a man in a straw hat is sharpening a machete on a boulder. He doesn't notice me walking by.

A car park with a lizard and an alleyway with a cat bring me to the beach and at last I can stand under the big palm trees. They're curtsying to a warm, wet blow from the sea. Sea-noise blots out all other sounds as waves the size of inter-state trucks pile past offshore rocks and fizzle out at my feet. I take off my shoes, and then notice that a gang of youths has materialised behind me. Is this the right or the wrong time to remember all those warnings against wandering around poor neighbourhoods. I'm wearing a gold watch and carrying posh shoes...but above all I'm a pale, well-fed foreigner. These youngsters turn out to be surfers, but on another dimension to the eternal consumer adolescents from the littorals of California or Australia with their thousand-dollar boards and designer baggies.

In this neighbourhood they have home-made and much-patched gear. They're probably the same penniless youth who play African drums behind Pelhourinho Square in the evenings, singing sambas, making a carnival of poverty. The ones to whom, if you're wise, you'll give 40 pence to look after and clean your car when you go shopping in the city. Kids with old eyes who can make a middle-aged gringo reporter, for instance, feel not quite grown up.

The tilting green sea – now that my eyes are adjusted to an oblique light – is dotted with dancing and disappearing figures. They're walking on the water. One grinning urchin ploughs ashore under a precipice of water on a refrigerator door (from the old man's wheelbarrow?) and far out, a skinny boy miraculously rides a wave between rocks, crouching just ahead of its crest and at last, matador-like, steps off onto the sand.

I'm not just impressed – I'm probably what some would call uplifted. I'm thinking of devoting the rest of my life to surfing. Besides, when it comes to refreshment for the spirit, the young surfers of Bahia beat TV evangelists every time. No contest.

Taken with a Dash of Lime

Vienna 1993

Like gilded naughty Vienna itself, coffee gossip among the elegant
frauen absent-mindedly slipping cake at five quid a slice to jaded
dachshunds at Hotel Sacher, holds up a delightfully foxed mirror
to Europe:

> Lime is alive and well on the streets and selling plutonium
> from the back of a Soviet army lorry...the scores of tarts
> who wave at cars on the Outer Ring of an evening are
> now so regimented they always turn out in identical rara
> outfits... refugees from the east really must be sent back,
> but in the meantime, they make great gardeners and
> cleaners even if they never turn up on time for work.

The old boy at the kiosk on Schwartzenberg Platz (bratwurst roll
and beer £2.50) winks at you over his bottles of ketchup and sweet
mustard and puts it another way: 'When anyone in Europe farts,
Vienna smells it first.'

The sausage man's words came back to haunt me when I went
down Harry Lime's sewer. Above, collapsing regimes in the east
were no doubt creating the sort of black economies that would give

Graham Greene's war profiteer a predatory sense of *déjà-vu*, but down in the old town sewerage system, crocodiles of tourists were scaring the rats. Forget Mozart, Beethoven and Schubert; put the Schönbrunn Palace, Belvedere and the Art Nouveau train station at Karlsplatz on hold: English-speaking visitors must first check out the sewers where Orson Welles was cornered at the end of *The Third Man*.

'It's that old film,' said a guide wearily. 'I think a lot of British and American tourists are quite surprised when they realise that Vienna isn't in black and white.'

On the other hand, what better way to approach the technicolour gold, verdigris and white marble of Baroque architecture, the rigid curlicues of Otto Wagner – or indeed the vivid faces and clothes of, say, Romanian flea-market gypsies – than by emerging from its monotonous sewer?

As for above ground aromas in Vienna… these are often worth seeking out. The historic centre is mostly for walkers, with boulevards and parks, so smells and sounds are not confined to the stink and raw diktat of the car. To the sound of bells, my stroll around St Stephen's Cathedral was through wafts of beer, bread, cakes and horses. In a corner, a black-fingernailed man in peasant clothes played Hungarian dances on a home-made fiddle.

For people from north, south and east, Vienna is the big Apfel, and there are plenty of new Viennese at the food and flea markets on Kettenbrückengasse. It's a short ride on the underground from Harry Lime's sewer, and from the Opera. Schubert composed *Winterreise* at number 6. Were he living in this neighbourhood today, I thought, emerging from the U-Bahn station to colourful crowds, violin music and the smell of spices, Franz's creative melancholy would be put at considerable risk.

Otto Wagner's gold-encrusted Art Nouveau apartments look down on Hungarians, Czechs, Slovaks, Poles, Romanians, Gypsies, Turks and stocky, working-class Austrians selling everything from second-hand lederhosen (about £40 a pair, complete with stains) to home-made sauerkraut. A gypsy woman in a multi-coloured skirt reaches into her box of scavenged oddments and offers me a 'pretty house ornament' for £12, a pot-metal bust of Hitler.

Resisting the temptation to search miles of fascinating old tat for more Adolfiana – as a young, unsuccessful art-student in Vienna it's said he churned out 'views' for a postcard company – I went in search of lunch.

Emperor ('I'm the Emperor and I want dumplings') Ferdinand set the ground-rules at the beginning at the century: serious grub and lots of it. What was described as an ordinary light lunch in the old outdoor restaurant near the Giant Wheel (yet another *Third Man* landmark) in the Prater fun park, turned out to be the best part of a pig's leg accompanied by a mound of potatoes with cream and salad, with horseradish, mustard, a crusty loaf and beer on the side. Conversation in Vienna often comes round to pesky gall bladders and the need to get them fixed.

Anyway, after that lunch l was not in best shape for the Prater's Sex Museum or Super Death Looper. Both really require a strong, unburdened stomach, but a reporter's gotta do what a reporter's gotta do, even when in anaconda-after-a-brace-of-warthog mode. After that, the 214-foot high Giant Wheel was a doddle, a refuge from G-strings and G-forces, recommendable for its views of the city.

Maybe it was the Big Lunch or the Sex Museum or both that made a subsequent encounter with Klimt's eroto-*Jugendstil* frieze at the Secession building a touch unsettling. Klimt's homage to Beethoven, Richard Wagner and Schiller shows a man whose pants appear to have fallen around his ankles. He's embracing a pale woman. A peeved person in a full suit of armour seems to be wishing he'd slipped into something a mite more comfortable. In the opulent severity of that building, it's like coming upon guests misbehaving at a posh party.

The high-camp white marble goings-on around a gilded Johann Strauss on his memorial in the Stadtpark seem positively suburban after Klimt. A perfect spot for a digestive nap. This linden-shaded monument to ballroom libido, I noticed with shock, has *no graffiti*! Back home, of course, I'd have to have been dreaming already.

I was warming to kitsch; it was time to seek out Mozart's grave. The Number 71 tram took me, armed with *Famous Graves in Vienna* by Professors Adler and Clemens (Perlen-Reihe, Vienna), to the Friedhof St Marx. In Mozart's time the place was a far-flung plague pit and pauper depository. In the last century or so he's been joined by upward classes creating a smashing example of what we would call High Victorian Gothic in what is still an unfashionable neighbourhood of high-rise flats, overpasses and the whiff of immigrant cooking.

If you haven't booked weeks (preferably months) in advance for a weekend concert, and you don't fancy a long queue for a standing-only ticket, you can always head for the Woods – a somewhat misleading name for the bosky vine terraces and villages that mark the last spasms of the Alps.

Schubert and his drinking pals used to drive out from the city by horse-drawn *fiaker* like the ones for hire around the Hofburg. The splendid electric trams, like the Number 41 that took me on the 40-minute ride from the Ring to within a short walk of Neustift am Walde, are no less romantic. And with a 72-hour pass (covering trams, buses and trains) costing about £7, cheap.

Heurige, the farmhouse pubs of wine villages like Neustift, still display fir branches over their doors to advertise new wine. The local white is refreshing, sharp and stronger than you thought, and the dinners strictly Ferdinand-style. My pub had: boiled beef with roast potatoes, beans and horseradish and apple (£8), blood sausage with sauerkraut (£3.50), apricot dumplings (£3). And people *waltzed* on this kind of thing?

The sun was going down and cicadas were starting to compete with the accordionist. 'Ach! I think you ate not lunch today!' said the dirndled waitress collecting a pile of empty plates from my table under the walnut tree and going off to fetch apricot brandy and coffee with whipped cream.

Everything is Tickety-Boo

TAMIL NADU 1994

(Is that a camera in your pocket or are you just...)

'Welcome. What is your good name? Mine is Baby,' says the blue-chinned beauty, tottering downstairs on sequined stilettos and grabbing me in a scented embrace.

We are in a clinch on the back stairs of a grotty hotel in a dog-eared town in Tamil Nadu. Baby is here with a posse of transsexuals. They – bejewelled, kohl-eyed and wafting in bright silk wedding saris – spotted me from the upstairs balcony. I, a passing foreigner on a motorbike, must have been an unlikely apparition under the blow-lamp midday sun. And fair game. They had whooped and hollered from their balcony. I had been intrigued.

Welcoming whoops and hollers from a hotel full of brides makes for a *carpe diem* situation if ever there was one. I had parked the elderly Rajdoot and climbed the stairs.

Baby leads me to the crowded balcony and I am hugged sweatily all round. Smiling faces are thrust against mine, knuckles held against my temples and, by painless sleight of hand, cracked loudly. 'It means very nice good luck,' Baby breathes in my ear. Baby and friends are constantly tweezering-away at persistent patches of face-stubble. I am the target for valedictory dabs of perfume. I begin to smell like the inside of a showgirl's handbag.

This activity is delighting locals in the street below and they are sending the odd raucous shout in my direction. I ignore them. Up here on the balcony, after all, I am a hit. 'We are liking your equipment,' says Baby, giving my Pentax a friendly prod.

Baby and friends call themselves *Ompatukal* - 'Number Nines', which they claim is a slang term popularised by a long-forgotten Bollywood movie. Officially known as *Alis* (Tamil) or *Hijra* (Hindi), India's Number Nines make up an informal caste that includes gays, transsexuals, transvestites and even hermaphrodites.

They are a brazen lot – contradictions inhabiting contradictory worlds – and much in demand both as prostitutes and performers of auspicious dances at weddings and birth celebrations. They often live as wives in what are regarded as marriages. They adopt children – usually from within their own or their partner's extended families.

These new friends of mine are on a pilgrimage. Arrived here from Pondicherry (half an hour down the road) and from Madras and from far away Delhi and Bombay for the two-day festival of *Koothandavar* at a nearby village, tomorrow they will dance themselves into trances and 'become' incarnations of Vishnu as a beautiful bride for a doomed prince. But now, in the last stages of pre-nuptial prink, they are all dressed up with nowhere to go... and nothing much to do except enrol me as their photographer. In a class of their own as far as narcissism, campery and sheer bitchiness go, my Number Nines are, nevertheless, radiant at the prospect of being avatars for the Protector of the Universe.

By posing like this for my camera, says Baby, they are making *puja*, a ritual offering. And by clicking the shutter I, it seems, am earning good karma points too. l was *meant* to come here on my motorbike to take their pictures; my next incarnation will reap the benefit. Karma-wise, they imply, this is a clear win win situation for me.

There is a lot of pushing and shoving as I focus on my unruly subjects. Through the lens I notice a statue of Gandhi in the road below. He seems to look on with an indulgent twinkle through thick bronze specs. A mynah bird lands on the saintly old fixer's polished head.

Then I am hauled into a cubicle-sized room to meet Nandini – or rather, to be shown Nandini's newly created female body. Smiling, Nandini – who usually is to be found in the *Ompatukal* enclave of Madras – yanks aside a green and pink Benares sari to reveal large breasts above and a long scar below. Lakshmi, an older transvestite, comes in, nods approvingly, and says 'Nandini is now beautiful. Not all have the courage which is necessary for this.'

About one in four *Ompatukal* endure crude operations to remove testes and penis. This is usually done without recourse to anaesthetic or antibiotics. The death rate is said to be one in ten.

Surrounded by such friendly faces, I don't feel like asking Baby what the Number Nines think of this month's article in *India Today* which, under the headline 'Eunuchs fight back' goes on about abductions and back yard castrations by a *Hijra* 'mafia'. 'Did it hurt?' I ask Nandini, lamely. Nandini's reply is lost in the sudden eruption of a screaming quarrel on the balcony.

I am reminded of pain-thresholds the next day as I ride into the village of Pillarikuppam. A festival like *Koothandavar* is not for the noise-sensitive, agoraphobic, or anyone less than enamoured of the colour orange. The half-dozen earth streets of this typical Tamil village are clamorous with out-of-sync shades of orange and seismic lo-fi Tamil music. Local men and boys as well as visiting *Ompatukal* are in full drag. Village wives help their transformed husbands choose glass wedding bangles from hawkers. Sunlight filters through the blue smoke of cooking fires. Kids squeal aloft on rickety, man-powered rides.

It's noisy and hot, and I am on the point of sneaking off with my mental snapshots (a siren voice in my head droning *Pondicherry, cold beer! Let's go!*) when I am nabbed by Lakshmi, Baby and co.

They have been at the palm wine. 'Everything,' announces Ramadas, a very old and dignified transexual whose makeup is beginning to run, 'is tickety-boo.'

At the *chai* shop, enjoying my umpteenth sugary tea, I am captured by a toddy-eyed policeman intent on giving me a foundation course in Gender Studies: 'Man into woman chop-chop, no problem; woman into man we are finding more tricky.' Six-foot Trimurthi from Delhi, in gorgeous black and gold silk sari, striped bodice, anklets, long earrings, nose-jewel and games-mistress manner, comes to my rescue.

'This is *puja* for me to tell you about Trimurthi,' says Trimurthi. 'I am 46 years old. My mother and father were poor labourers. From earliest days I liked women's work such as cleaning and I wanted to dress as woman. I developed interest in boys.'

'At 17 years I ran away and married a man. I was in love. We brought up two boys as our sons. They are now married and I have two grandchildren. They call me mother. My husband died seven years ago. l never see my parents or my brother and sister. Where I live in Delhi there are about 50 of us and we dance for a living. We earn about 1,000 rupees (£21) a month but it can be double this. Tamil Nadu is not a good place for *Hijras* and we only come for the festival. Here we feel out of station.'

When the sun goes down, Trimurthi, Baby, Lakshmi, Nandini, Ramadas and the others, dance by the light of flares in front of the village temple. They are crazed-looking, avid, with dilated eyes and bared teeth. There is unremitting drumming from *parais* (the Tamil drum), invariably played by men of the lowest caste – and hence the wellspring of our word 'pariah') and the raw squealing of reed trumpets. The atmosphere is charged. Twirling dancers' saris brush a villager slumped hiccupping against the temple wall. He vomits toddy. This is Kuttandavar's wedding night.

Next morning the show goes on. The flower-draped idol of Prince Kuttandavar – by now, according to legend, having met his end on the battlefield – is drawn on a huge wagon from the temple to a field outside the village. At each halt devotees break their glass wedding bangles against the vehicle. The great wheels are badged with the blood of sacrificial goats.

At last, the din begins to tail off. People are taking flowers from the cortege and setting off for home. The Number Nines have changed out of their wedding finery for the plain white dresses of widowhood. On my way to the motorbike I am informed that Parvati wants to see me.

Parvati – young and pretty, with a studied, tragic expression, makes a dramatic appearance in the doorway of a village hut. To reach the threshold I have to step over the sleeping bodies of families who have rented out the house for the festival. Parvati smiles at my famous camera. 'Actually, I'm not a *pukka* photographer,' I start to say as, inside the hut, Parvati whips off the widow's shift and strikes a bizarre Pirelli Calendar nudie pose.

I click away. Parvati says dreamily, 'Twelve days I was sick when I was made woman. Forty days before I walk again. This was nine years ago. I went from Madras with three others to a village in Andhra Pradesh. We each had to pay 10,000 rupees and bring five kilos of oil. The oil was heated and put on our cuts. All the time I am praying to Mataji the Mother God. After the cut I feel happy. I was 16.' Parvati's pre-operation name was Purushottaman which means 'best among men.'

The old motorbike starts first kick. Baby, there to see me off with a final knuckle crunch and dab of musk, says, 'And we are all hoping that your research has been of the satisfactory variety.' 'Tickety-boo,' I say.

Facing the Flood Gates

INDIA 1994

Stepping out of the dugout canoe that has carried her across the Narmada River in this remote corner of western India where Gujarat, Maharashtra and Madhya Pradesh meet, Medha Patkar clips a pen to her sari, picks up two heavy bags, and sets out on a five-hour walk to another tribal village. She turns down an offer to carry her bags, explaining, with a schoolgirl giggle: 'We make a point of carrying our own baggage – that way the villagers won't mistake us for government officials.'

Not that there's much chance of that. Medha is the inspiration behind a movement that could turn one of the world's biggest dam-building projects into an embarrassing white elephant for the Indian government. Over the last ten years she has become a legendary figure in this remote region of denuded hills, encouraging *Bhil* tribespeople to resist plans to shift them from their ancestral lands. The multi-billion-dollar Narmada Dam project calls for the inundation of 119 settlements by a 500-kilometre-long lake that will be deep enough to cover Cologne Cathedral. An estimated 200,000 tribespeople would have to be re-settled, 'and there just isn't the land, the money or the will available to compensate them all,' claims Medha.

Already, the base for the main dam is in place, and despite court orders, contractors this year closed the first sluices. With the coming of the Monsoon, Narmada waters have started to engulf low-lying fields and villages.

'Now that they want to evict us,' – and the 'us' comes quite naturally from this social sciences graduate from worlds-away Bombay – 'government officers and police have started coming into the area. Before that they didn't know or care where the villages were.' Medha has threatened, along with many villagers, to stay put and drown rather than leave the area.

Forty-one years old, five feet nothing in her cheap canvas slippers and with thick grey-flecked hair framing the face of a happy, mischievous child, Medha is hardly the stereotype for a class warrior or eco-commando. At first, she walked the Narmada valley alone. Now she has six helpers. Together they make the active heart of Narmada Bachao Andolan, the Save Narmada Group, and operate out of a cubby-hole office above a dairy.

'You're lucky to find me,' Medha had said when I rang her Baroda number to ask for an interview. 'We've just had a visit from local political *goondhas* (thugs) and the office is well...all smashed up. The only thing they didn't destroy was a picture of Gandhi.' There was a chuckle from the other end of a bad line. 'Come along by all means...but this line's bugged, so *everybody* will be expecting you.'

Perhaps they were. Certainly, in Baroda, a police jeep was parked outside my hotel. When I phoned Medha again she said: 'Better not come to the office – these days the place is surrounded by police...and they'll think you're one of those foreign subversives our politicians are always talking about.' Our Famous Five-type stratagem was to meet on a busy street.

As she emerged from the passing throng and slipped into my elderly Ambassador taxi, she was amused by the fact that our cover appeared to have been well and truly blown: two police jeeps appeared suddenly out of the traffic chaos and fell into line behind us as we drove out of town.

'The official line is that we have made ourselves so unpopular that we have to be protected,' Medha explained, and leading a convoy of bored-looking policemen, we drove past fields of cotton towards the border and the homelands of the *Bhil*.

Conceived half a century ago, the Narmada Dam scheme, it is claimed, will supply India's parched western areas by about the year 2000, and transform the lives of millions of poor farmers. Irrigation and drinking water would benefit four states and even reach the salty wilderness of the Rann of Kutch, on the border with Pakistan.

The full, grandiose scheme of 30 large and more than 100 small dams could go on well into the 21st century. Gujarat Dam Association has promised: 'Every relocated family will be given a new home, electricity, water on tap and initial financial support...we will free the *Bhil* from poverty.'

Medha, together with some Indian experts, believes that the scheme would be disastrous for tribals and others displaced by the rising water and planned canal infra-structure. The only beneficiaries, they think, will be an elite, already-wealthy minority.

Both sides of the debate have assembled exhaustive (not to say exhausting) arguments to support their points of view. But there can be no doubt that the pro-dam factions suffered a serious blow last year when an independent study led the World Bank – originally a prime-mover in the dam project and contributor of 450 million dollars – and the Indian government to terminate loan agreements. It was clear that ecological and resettlement conditions for further loans could not be met. Politicians blamed international anti-Indian influences – and Medha.

Bitterness has entered the dispute. Anti-dam demonstrators have been beaten and jailed – at least one killed – by state police. Promises to complete the project, and references to sinister foreign plots, have become a staple of local electoral rhetoric.

This year, court orders and previous undertakings were ignored as sluices on the dam's lower level were closed, raising the level of the Narmada and submerging about 50 tribal farmhouses.

The National government, meanwhile, have begun targeting investment from expatriate Indian communities abroad. Published estimates for the cost of completion of the scheme vary with partisan wildness from 5 to 13 billion dollars.

In 1991 Medha travelled to Stockholm to receive the Alternative Nobel Prize. She thinks now the award might have done more harm than good to her cause. Although Medha refused to accept the cash part of the award, Indian politicians have accused her of being swayed by foreign influence and money. 'The truth is, we always turn down offers of money so we can't be accused of not being a genuine grassroots organisation.

'We don't have any money. Next month, when some of us take the train to Delhi to protest about the illegal closing of the sluices, we'll be travelling ticketless. We have to set out early so that if we get put off, we can catch another train.'

Our police escort stayed with us until we ran out of blacktop road. At what used to be the far-flung village of Kothi and is now a surreal high-rise development for dam technicians and workers, we swapped our taxi for an even more clapped-out jeep. From then on, we drove on earth, only occasionally meeting laden timber lorries. They crawled behind us in the red clouds of dust that veiled a low sun.

Bottom-numbing hours later we were alone among trackless river-beds and forested hills where much get-out-and-shove was called for, and we reached the Narmada long after sunset. At last, we climbed out and stretched our limbs in the refreshing silence.

Stars lit our way up a hillside towards the cooking-fires of a *Bhil* settlement and we stooped through the doorway of a big wooden building with a thatch and tile roof. The forms of squatting people and of curious-eyed white cattle emerged from the darkness. We were welcomed by Indya and his wife Budhi.

In a city street, Indya's dark, tattooed face, splayed-toes and tousled hair, would mark him out as an uncomfortable example of primitive poverty. At home in his teak and bamboo farmhouse, surrounded by three generations of his family and their precious animals, he becomes a lord in his own domain and a generous host.

Taking down a huge reaping-knife from the wall, Indya shaves fragrant slices of green mango for us. We are given tea – a rare luxury in these hills – and Budhi looks after the cooking of millet bread which we devour with raw onions and cane-sugar *jaggery*.

'My family have always lived in this place,' said Indya, 'although the government says we have to show ownership papers. When the water rises, we'll just have to take these house-timbers and move to higher ground.'

A pair of fish-eagles quartered the river as we set out in log canoes the next morning. On either side were the same tawny hills and little stands of dry trees. The only clue to the fact that we were within a day's march of where bulldozers were going about their enormous business, was the widening river itself. We crossed to the far shore, into Maharashtra, and immediately set off on foot. 'No time for swimming,' said Medha, who must have been reading my mind. 'We must get on...and there are big crocodiles in there.'

The government has made promises it can't possibly keep, alleges Medha, offering money and land-for-land: 'There just isn't enough comparable land to re-settle all these people, so the government is giving smaller amounts of unsuitable land – even ousting other tribals to provide it – and claiming that many of the people here are illegal squatters and therefore not eligible for compensation.'

In the three-house settlement of Mukdhi, old Ranya Daya takes a few puffs on the communal water-pipe and says: 'I have three sons and seven daughters and I have my animals and five acres of hillside to grow food. We can gather *mahwah* blossoms to make wine, we have fish in the river and wood in the forest. Old papers prove that this land is ours. But the land the government wants us to take is not so good and it's smaller. Now the water is rising and soon the monsoon will come. We are hoping she (a calloused, claw hand indicates Medha) will find out some medicine for this problem.'

We set off again, this time into a blazing hot afternoon. Before long, catching sight of the river, I flee down a stony defile desperate for a drink. I'd long ago abandoned all attempts to avoid 'drinking the water'; in fact, I'd even decided that Narmada water was infinitely superior to the bottled stuff I'd been subsisting on. As I stand wiping my chin, a long-haired man clad only in a bright yellow cod-piece, appears. He materialises from around a large rock, carrying a trident and a gourd, at the same time as a tiny, dark metallic bird hovers out of a flowering bush. 'Nice!,' says the naked man, in unexpected English, giving me a bright smile and striding off downriver.

'You've just met a holy man – a *sadhu* – on a pilgrimage,' they tell me when I catch up with the group. For many devotees of Shiva, the Narmada is the holiest river in India. Pilgrims walk the whole length of the river – 1,380 kilometres – and then back on the other side. 'It's supposed to take them three years, three months and three days,' says Medha, '…not like our little walk.'

Nevertheless, our 'little walk' lasted well into the next night and we had to wade in the Narmada to round a headland. *Bhil* villagers set straw fires to guide us up the last dark hillside. We stumbled into the village of Pepulchup and a waiting crowd of more than 200 burst into a song of welcome. I learned later that many of the villagers had walked for days to be there.

I was too weary to eat, and collapsed on a *charpoy*. The last thing I remember before falling asleep was seeing Medha, relaxed and tireless, talking to a spellbound crowd against a background of stars.

Morning in Pepulchup begins with the rumble of querns: grain being turned into meal. Women in short green saris, one corner draped over their heads, fetch water from the river. A clear, horizontal light picks out maize stubble and the red leaves of the *mahwah* trees. Fruit bats return from their raids and kingfishers whizz along the encircling fingers of the Narmada.

We are 200 kilometres from the nearest town of any size, I reflect, as a small gang of fascinated children watch me sip a cup of tea. Explosions can be heard from far across the river where gypsum is being torn out of the Gujarat hills – providing cement for the dam. I am wondering if the villagers of Pepulchup will share the fate of the people of Manibeli, a slightly lower village not far from the dam site. There, already, villagers have been forced to leave, many being sent to live in temporary tin sheds in areas with little or no water, fuel or grazing. According to Medha and her helpers – who admit that some *Bhil* have been glad to move towards mainstream Indian society – half of the Manibeli oustees no longer own cows or goats. Eighty per-cent of them have become debtors.

A barefoot girl plucks up courage and comes over to show me her school slate. I have been watching 14 pupils having lessons under the village's 100-year-old tamarind tree in the cool hours just after dawn. The school, the region's first, was started a couple of years ago by Narmada Bachao Andolan. Beyond the children is a brightening landscape of hills and rising water. In neat Marathi script, this pupil has written: 'My name is Sampat and my abode is Pepulchup. Long live India!'

Searching for Blue Eyes

Unstoppable, like one of Rommel's *Panzers*. Tall, blonde, wearing nothing much but boots and a bum-length fur coat. She strode through falling snow and rapped on the car.

'Wilkommen in Hamburg, Jonny!' she had said, fixing me with ironic blue eyes as I wound down the window and tried to explain that this evening I wasn't looking for companionship – I wanted directions to a place called Hans Albers Platz. 'Let's be friends just for tonight on the Reeperbahn...,' she had sung huskily in my ear, and an icy wind had carried the refrain away over the cobbles of the fish market.

I was reminded of Mitzi when I returned to Hamburg recently and from the juke-box in a bar called La Paloma, found myself listening to the same ditty. A middle-aged couple linked arms at the bar and were singing along, swaying to the oompah rhythm. 'He's very popular here,' said the bar-boy with the eye-liner and the slicked-down retro haircut, polishing a glass. 'He sang it in one of his films... it's Hans Albers.' Intriguing, I thought, to find out years later that Mitzi might not after all have been extending an invitation when she'd crooned for me in the fish market. She could simply have been referring to this Hans What's-his-name who'd had a Platz named after him. Of such stuff are bar-room epiphanies made.

Walk up from Landungsbrücken or down from St Pauli station and Hans Albers Platz is as good a place as any to set off from on an exploration of the old harbour areas. On this occasion I had time to notice the light-hearted Expressionist-style memorial to Albers, showing him in merchant sailor's uniform, with an accordion, and with a bronze seagull perched on his cap. My search for a plaque was soon being interrupted by solicitations from local tarts who all wear knickers outside of their bodysuits à la Steve Bell's John Major carica-ture. A sound as of elephant-seals in rut had started to emanate from the Union flag bedecked English Pub across the way. It was time to flee.

Many of the enormous old apartment blocks between the Elbe and the Reeperbahn have been occupied for years now by Alternative Youth, becoming totally mural-ised in the process. Separate buildings are dedicated, inside and out, to political, artistic and sexual minorities. There's even one – for, presumably, unclassifiable tenants – known as Chaos House.

Crossing the Reeperbahn I found myself on Wohlwillstrasse looking through a run-down shop window at a painting: a blue-eyed sailor playing an accordion and wearing a cap on which perched a seagull. It was Hans Albers. Clearly, I would have to buy it. Inside, I met Karlo Kannibalo and his dog Lupo who run what Karlo calls a 'people's gallery for cheap art'. The unframed work on the walls, painted with decorator's colours on materials rescued from skips, is the work of Karlo and others signing themselves 'KK', 'Deutschmark Bob', 'Sam' and '4000' – '4000' has a 'not half so good' imitator who signs himself, appropriately, '2000'. The Albers painting, with Karlo's signature 'K' on the seaman's cap, cost £15. Not bad, it seemed to me, for such a big one. Kannibalo started out as plain Karl Hilse, son of a Ruhr steelworker, in Gelsenkirchen – 'I think it is the same as your Milton Keynes so you see it was necessary for me to get out...in Hamburg we have a better atmosphere for making art and also I discover here Hans Albers, a hero for me.'

'Is there anything else I can tell you about Hamburg?' said Bezirksamtsleiter (District Office Manager) Jochen von Maydell after he'd explained the city's recession-beating strategies of diversification away from heavy industries, and the way Hamburg's refugees – the city takes care of more than the entire UK total – are being encouraged out of ethnic ghettos and into mainstream life in the new Germany. 'What about Hans Albers?' I asked. 'He seems to crop up all the time.' It was, said von Maydell, a good question (I had feared it might be a darned fool one) because there was something about Albers – a butcher's son who became a movie star during the Hitler era – that was essentially Hamburg.

'Not just because he was born here and lived most of his life here, and spoke with a Hamburg accent, but because he always seemed to play himself – an ordinary, decent chap, weak, fond of drink and ladies, and who responded to Fate's cruelties with a song. A romantic loser. One who sails away. One who doesn't get the girl in the last reel.'

When the talkies came along, Hans' man-in-the-strasse image and his piano-bar singing voice were in great demand by a regime that was keen to promote 'Aryan'-looking artists. But (and here life, perhaps, started to imitate celluloid tragedy) Albers' wife was a Jew. She had to leave Germany.

Hans went on to become famous for his boozy, fatalistic irony. And as he sang about making the most of life on the Reeperbahn – then, as now, one of the world's most notorious red-light areas – the world exploded. Among other things, Britain's airborne attack on Hamburg, Operation Gomorrah, in one night killed 42,000 civilians, destroying in the process eight square miles of the city. The Alster Lake boiled.

Babylon. It makes you think of Babylon, the amazingly solid, tiered and intricate brickwork of the Expressionist architect Fritz Höger. His 1920s *Chilehaus* (the money for it came from the Chilean saltpetre trade) is built in the shape of an ocean-going ship. Emerging from the U-Bahn at Messberg station and catching sight of this extraordinary building, I wondered if Hans Albers had seen the *Chilehaus* as it must have been on a night in 1943, sailing a sea of rubble on a wind of fire. The fleeting comforts and imperfect pianos of the Reeperbahn might well have seemed like souvenirs of a lost Shangri-La after that. As von Maydell had said: 'Supermen mess up the world. Ordinary people have a delightful tendency to elect alternative heroes who are fallible, sentimental, funny. Entertainers like Hans Albers, maybe.' Amen.

All this *Sturm* and *Drang* was making me peckish. From the *Chilehaus* I went in search of lunch and, thanks to Cornelius, a Hamburg artist who paints portraits of the rich and consequently has to eat with the poor – I found the tax office canteen in Steinstrasse. I suspect that the place is meant for government employees only, but at the moment they still welcome all comers and do a great line in plain German food: smoked pork, sauerkraut, potato salad – that sort of thing – for £2. The canteen is round the corner from the *Chilehaus* in the basement of an Art Deco ministry building that looks like an early wireless with some severe cornucopias stuck on the side. Hurry, before the tax office realises it's been rumbled.

Give or take a few severe cornucopias and the like, the buildings of Hamburg are always interesting and quite often beautiful, which is unexpected when you know that as well as suffering Operation Gomorrah the city centre was totally consumed by the Great Fire 100 years before. And, as one of the world's wealthiest cities (even today it has the highest per-capita income in Germany) the place has always been fertile ground for vogueish architectural adventures. I even heard it said that grandiose civic schemes had been more destructive of historic buildings than the firestorms of 1842 and 1943 combined. The salutary, blackened neo-Gothic stump of the church of St Nikolai which replaced a real Gothic structure, has been left as a reminder of war.

Today, Hamburg's skyline combines some wonderful Art Deco and Expressionist survivals, surprising clusters of still busy, richly decorated 19th-century brick warehouses, interspersed with Modern Prestige High-tech. The city plants 2,000 trees every year.

With its greenery and parks, its lakes and canals, Hamburg – population 1.7 million and growing – doesn't look like Germany's second biggest industrial centre after Berlin. 'We had to be prepared, ever since the 1970s, to make radical changes, socially and industrially,' said von Maydell who, clearly, is pleased with the way things are going.

Hamburg remains a work-hard, play-hard sort of place. The ancient ship-building industry has given way to specialised re-fit work. Hamburg is where the *Queen Elizabeth* goes for multi-million-dollar check-ups. *Spiegel, Zeit, Stern, Bild Zeitung* are all published here and Hamburg's aircraft servicing industry is the world's biggest after Seattle. There are signs that the port is becoming once again the main western gateway for the Baltic trade. Hans Albers' red-light area, St Pauli, now sees more tourists than punters, and the 1,700 official, tax-paying good-time girls are suffering a down-turn in trade – a result of the changing requirements of visitors and a big influx of unofficial sex-workers from the ex-Soviet countries.

Walking with throngs of tourist families around the Hafen and fish market area, I wondered how the cold winds of change might have affected Mitzi in her poignantly short fur coat.

Some things don't change in Hamburg. Down in the Free Port area you'll crunch cacao and coffee beans underfoot on the big grey cobbles, and the beautiful warehouses still hold caliphs' ransoms of oriental carpets, although these days the odiferous treasure usually comes overland rather than by ship. In the back streets, dark-featured drivers squat beside their parked Iranian lorries, fingering oily stews of peppers and beans. It's reckoned that at any one time, Hamburg's warehouses are holding carpets worth 1.5 billion deutschmarks.

Within a salivating stroll of all those spicy carpets (not to mention the delicious-looking pickled aubergines that one driver was packing away) is another of Cornelius' favourite food stops. 'You can't miss it,' he'd said, 'because it looks like a flying turn-of-the-century municipal lavatory that has made a bad landing.'

It did. The *Oberhafen-Kantine* is the size of an average cricket pavilion (or, if you prefer, a large public toilet) and leans improbably towards the railway that passes overhead, as if looking for support. It's a gem: a small 'unimportant' public building that has managed to survive for 100 years or so without being updated, painted or otherwise messed about.

The *Kantine* was built to provide cheap and solid beer lunches for dockers. I walked through the wonky door, sat down at a sloping table under some angled and very full flypapers, and called for beer. The old barman and Marianne the cook both – like the flypapers – fit so perfectly with the place you begin to suspect the whole set-up might be an avant-garde theatre project...that any minute a man with a pony-tail and a megaphone might appear at the table and say: 'God! Not with that tie! Please!' But nobody noticed me as I tackled *Bauernfrühstück mit Schinken und Gurke* which, with beers, came to about £4. I paid up and left quickly before any guys with ponytails spotted me, or the *Kantine* took flight for the Milky Way, or I woke up. Also, I wanted to go shopping for a shrunken head.

It's in St Pauli, on Bernhard-Nocht-Strasse, the shrunken-head shop. At least it used to sell shrunken heads, and much else besides according to my informant who haunted the place as a boy. And it certainly is a proper junk shop...difficult to miss because it spills out onto the pavement to meet you. The owner resembles The Ancient Mariner. For years he's bought curiosities from visiting sailors. And clearly, he's one of those junk dealers who can't bear to part with anything. Now the stock occupies six houses behind the road. If a person had time, they would find a shrunken head or two... at least.

After that it was time to drop in at the Museum of Erotic Art at number 69. Forty originals by Picasso, Cocteau, Grosz and the like. A room by Tomi Ungerer where unsuspecting visitors can be goosed by the steel and leather furniture. Four magnificent large paintings of Amsterdam hookers by Volker Stelzmann. Henry Miller has some water-colours which are nowhere near as *al dente* as his prose. You can be startled, going up the narrow stairs, by encountering with your hand a huge hank of human hair on the banister. It's all good unclean fun and I liked the way the butch, room-dividing chains (the place is an old warehouse), after a while started to take on a pleasing ambiguity. A nice touch: the plain brown paper bags used for purchases in the museum book shop.

The City Art Museum (*Kunsthalle*, near the main railway station) looks like a Victorian wedding-cake – which doesn't quite prepare you for some of the bathtub-becomes-Art-because-I-say-it-does modernity of Josef Beuys or, for that matter, the wonderful Expressionist collection. Oskar Kokoschka's impressions of Hamburg harbour stood up well to my fresh memories of the real thing. My favourite picture is the portrait of Egon Erwin Kisch by Christian Schad. Kisch, a respected between-the-wars Hamburg journalist, is posed without his shirt, so that we can see – beneath his urbane exterior – an *outré* collection of tattoos. A very Hamburg combination.

Doing the Free-Market Mazurka

Warsaw 1994

You wonder how strenuous activity like this can produce such splendid melancholy. Looked at from behind, the pianist's elbows are as energetic as a washer-woman's. At the buzzy old Steinway under the concert-salon chandeliers of the Myślewicki Palace, she's wringing, out of Chopin's Polonaise in A-flat major, the sound of bombers. We have swaying meadows, cavalry, a glissando of falling bricks. It's a very Warsaw experience.

At the City Museum it costs a quid to see a film of the destruction of Warsaw during the 1944 German retreat. Arpeggios of dynamite explosions followed by fire...until a city which rivalled Paris looks exactly like Hiroshima after the atom bomb. The Myślewicki Palace and its *belle époque* music room where we sit on hard chairs and feel the outside chill creeping in, was spared. It had housed Luftwaffe Command. Chopin himself performed here. I imagine him peeping out from under that Bosie-ish cowlick upon these same window-illuminated lawns and the iron railings that look as if they could stop a tank.

For a hard-currency crowd at a posh bash in today's post-Soviet Europe, tonight's concert-goers are surprisingly short in the gangster and briefcase departments. No accoutremental bimbos. We look like a bourgeois audience from before the War. No one has flashed a wad, a gun or an electronic organiser, or bawled for vodka. Maybe things are looking up.

Of course, it could simply mean that in Warsaw the new money doesn't go in for old music – although what better metaphor for today's lurching 'I'm alright, Jerzy!' capitalism than one of Chopin's more disorderly mazurkas?

In the interval there's sparkling wine and muted conversation in a dusty, elegant conference room under the beady eye of King Stanisław. His painted gaze follows you wherever you go. Old Stan would have been impressed by the expertise of his Stalin-era Foreign Ministry successors who so infested the room with electronic bugs that, at one conference with Korea, not a word was uttered as notes were passed around and then burned at the white marble fireplace.

The big square building on Jerozolimskie Avenue where all those bug wires led – Communist Party HQ – has become (what else?) a Stock Exchange. Around Bank Square, which used to commemorate dreaded Dzerzhinsky of the KGB, the double-parked Mercs are extremely apolitical. Today we are talking strictly readies, Comrade. 'It's 100 per cent certain in Soviet time this conversation is bugged,' a Warsaw friend had said when we'd chatted in my hotel room. It was quite possible it was happening now, he said (and we stared thoughtfully at the room's mirrors and newly decorated walls) but people were no longer afraid. 'We can say what we like…interest today is in commercial operations, industrial secrets, money.' Nice to know, I told my friend, that the bums and jobless who now shelter in Warsaw Central station are as free as their Western counterparts to bad-mouth the government.

Dissonant omens of aeroplane engines in that 150-year-old Opus 53 made me think of Bruno Schultz, shot dead in a Polish street in 1942 when he left a ghetto to look for bread. Schultz's writings of the 1920s, in some eerie inter-textual way, anticipated the awfulness to come. In *The Street of Crocodiles* there's always something atavistic behind the wallpaper. Schultz would have recognised, too, the tragic comedy of a regime that needed to censor even sports reports. Around 50,000 civilians died defending Warsaw in the 1944 uprising. Children wearing scavenged German helmets took to the sewers and were overcome by starving rats as Stalin's 'liberation' forces looked on from across the Vistula and let the German army finish razing the city. The historic centre has been rebuilt with such extraordinary attention to detail – old photos and even Canaletto panoramas were used for reference – that it's hard to believe these aren't the same stones walked upon by Copernicus. The Heroes' Monument even has a rash of bullet-holes which, I was assured by my English-speaking friend, were 'courtesy of your Mr Black Decker.' Poles, he said, like to get the details right.

Stefan Gradowski as a returnee from London, now runs five restaurants and reckons to serve 4,000 meals a day. Getting it right for Stefan has not just been a matter of making sure that Boris Yeltsin had 'a lot' of vodka (and when a Pole talks about 'a lot' of vodka I'm impressed!) with his dinner: 'We are working from zero service tradition. I no sooner train someone they get snaffled by another outfit. Truffles, Dom Perignon, caviar I can get, but good waiters?'

I was hanging out with the big spenders in Stefan's impressive flagship operation, the Belvedere, the old Royal Orangery in Łazienki Park, and toying with roast veal and wild mushrooms. In the bad old days this was a good place to bring the kids – a public building where you could sit in the warm and look at the plants and the aquarium. Now it attracts the folks my friend calls 'ones-who-aren't-in-jail-yet.' A state school-teacher would blow more than a week's wages on dinner in order to check out the guppies and the lemon trees.

It's possible to eat very well indeed in Warsaw, for a price, and for the equivalent of two or three pounds there's now McDonald's and Burger King and the (extremely popular) pizza joints. But paying hard currency prices doesn't always guarantee post-Soviet service or decent grub. Some places where, in the grey old days, *apparatchiks* grazed, are not all going with the free-market flow...which can be fun if you like impenetrable gravy, waitresses with attitude and surreal hunting-lodge décor out of a Mario Lanza film. One unreconstructed eatery with high prices and triumphal boozing by suits with briefcases, was reminiscent – smells of old carpet and tinned spaghetti – of a church basement refuge. All it needed was a vicar called Dave.

Our guide for the Wilanów Palace was not best pleased that we – with what to her no doubt seemed decadent Western attitudes towards official time-tables – turned up late. For a few moments I thought I knew what it must be like to walk out onto a rugger field and face someone wearing the All-Black strip. She was almost dancing the *Haka*. I managed to salvage a few points by appreciating paintings – Géricaults and a huge David of someone petulant in yellow tights astride a lovingly rendered horse – but was sternly tutted-at for not keeping a straight face under a painted ceiling that featured an over-endowed male nude the size of a small whale. 'I think I have to keep my eye on you, bad boy,' announced the guide, who (despite the wink she gave me) really did have a Secret Police knack of creeping up on a person. I slunk off to the back of the group.

To the beautiful (on the inside) Grand Theatre of Opera and Ballet, at a bargain £4, for the Polish premiere of Penderecki's *Paradise Lost,* and am intrigued to see Satan banged up in a sort of floating cage in the form of a Mercedes radiator badge. When Adam and Eve are banished from the Garden, they wander off towards a bogglingly huge set like a view of the unfashionable left bank of the Vistula, with distant high-rises and industrial twilight... rather like the place I headed for next day, following rumours of bargains to be had at the open-air market in the suburb of Braga.

It's ironic that this semi-officially tolerated market has taken over a football stadium built to commemorate the tenth anniversary of the Communist Revolution. Here you can find bogus Levis, porn videos and sizzling 'Hot Dogis' with the strangely delicious aroma of overheated Bakelite. Debutant capitalists come here in fumy old Eastern Bloc cars and with suitcases tied with string to spread their offerings on the ground. There are a lot of car-parts, Russian dolls and fur hats. 'Are they real amber, or plastic?' I asked a Lithuanian, whose stock of yellow bead necklaces was piled up on an old newspaper. He shrugged and pulled his woolly hat further down against the freezing wind. Well, at five US dollars for six necklaces, I wasn't going to complain anyway, but after my flight home I tested one of the beads in a match-flame. Expecting the deadly whiff of plastic, I was rewarded with the incense of prehistoric forests.

Going Loco with the Gricers

'Some people might think that I'd wasted my life,' Mike says as the maize fields of Moldavia file past our carriage window in a haze of coal-smoke and steam. 'After all, I'm a 50-plus trainspotter who still lives with his mum in Bognor!'

In fact, and whatever the rest of the world might think, Mike Hudson's appreciation of the value of time – like that of his fellow enthusiasts – is finely tuned almost to the point of obsession. It's all part of what is probably the grandest passion, after the weather and angling, of the English-speaking world: railways.

'Interest seems to tail off the farther you go from middle Britain and the cradle of the Industrial Revolution,' says Mike. 'The French are more interested in food, for example, and you just don't seem to find any Italian trainspotters...of course it's very big in the old Brit colonies.'

I had fallen in with a train-load of British and Australian rail-buffs. Night and day the corridors of our luxury special train, on a steam-hauled progress from Kyiv to Sebastopol and back, were astir with stop-watches and time-tables and tales of heavy metal. These folk were dedicated 'gricers' – a term, apparently, based on the word 'grouse' and signifying one who 'bags' things. They are an instructive lot and if the Russian engineers were thinking of another swap – an FD20-2714 Nemirov-built 2-10-2 loco for one of the equally old, equally scruffy TE 2-10-0s left behind in the German retreat of World War 2, say – or if the last consignment of ex-Soviet coal left something to be desired quality-wise, I was certainly going to find out all about it.

It was catching, this virus. Soon I was slipping along to the bar of an evening for two-bottle discussions on (for me) exotic gricer topics such as de-clinkering procedures, horsepower, slippage and momentum ratios on track gradients, or the usefulness of potatoes for curing leaks in steam boilers.

I tutted with the best of them over the loss to world civilisation of British steam-age punctuality (spot-on to within a quarter of a minute, apparently). Before long I, too, fretted at yet another unexplained halt in some nameless ex-Soviet marshalling yard. I quietly pooh-poohed the official Russian assurance that the next type of engine put on would prove more serviceable than the last. I was to be heard speculating about the sort of bribe our trip organiser was having to employ to help local railway bosses remember where they kept the keys to their water-towers. Over warm Crimean champagne in the bar I demanded to know why we weren't heroically on schedule like those tatty, broken-windowed Moscow expresses squealing past in the opposite direction.

Mike Hudson looked glumly at the bar's *Apparat*-kitsch clock – in the form of a giant Rolex watch – and revealed that wonky schedules were messing-up his plans: 'I'm what they call a steam track-basher, which means that for me the whole point of coming on a trip like this is to actually observe the route.

'So long as we are moving, under steam, in daylight, I can draw a red line on the map which means I've 'done' that particular stretch... at night I have to make a dotted line which, if things go according to plan, I hope to convert to a red line on the way back.'

There were enthusiasts for every aspect of railwayana said Mike. Some were devoted to cataloguing all those dismal little cast-iron wotsits beside the tracks. Some, with the single-mindedness of collies, were rounding up rivet patterns around the world. Others felt the urge to eavesdrop with stereo sound recorders on assignations between engines and viaducts. And there were those who awaited with their camcorders the coming of sun angle, smoke direction and track curvature in one climactic train-filled 'glint' shot. But track-bashing, he thought, was probably as close as anyone could come to a pure unencumbered rail experience.

Such philosophising was all very well, but wouldn't it need a team of Jesuits to figure out the minimum light conditions necessary to 'see' a rail journey? And wouldn't Mike's dawn-to-dusk red line on the map be compromised by, for instance, a visit to the loo? 'We say that being able to distinguish the colour of grass constitutes acceptable red-line conditions,' said Mike, 'although we still haven't resolved the difficult matter of moonlight. And as for calls of nature, I usually wait until the terrain is right – where I have a good far ahead view – and then I make sure to get back from the lavatory before the train is too far along.'

Mike has been through Peru's railway system a couple of times without ever finding time to visit the ruins of Machu Picchu – 'but I did manage to fit in the Taj Mahal once when I was track-bashing in India. It's a matter of luck – track comes before tourism, steam before stomach.'

For rail enthusiasts of all persuasions – and they are probably the most-travelled group of people you could hope to find – it's the journey alone that matters. Quite a few that I spoke to on the Crimea Express had only a passing interest (literally) in what life was like beyond the world's rail networks. Mike Hudson – his regrettable snub to Inca architecture notwithstanding – is a notable exception. Not for him the hit-and-run gricing of Petey the Aussie number-cruncher who told me: 'Get the serial-numbers and run, that's the ticket…the world's our olive, mate, and we're out to stuff it.'

Although he doesn't readily admit it, Mike has learned to get by in most European languages. And he turned out to be a reliable source of background info on the ex-Soviet lands we were steaming through. Of course, he'd been there a few times before. Throughout nearly all of his working life, starting as a ticket clerk at Barnham Junction until early retirement this year from the Passenger Train Running Section at Redhill, Mike has managed to fit in five two-week track-bashing trips every year, seeking out steam routes wherever time and money would allow. This year he'd already been to Germany, Austria, Switzerland, France, Belgium, Italy and southern Poland.

Track-bashing being limited by daylight, in winter months Mike has to look farther afield – to South America, the Philippines, India…wherever steam engines still chuff: 'Maybe it's time to go back to New Zealand – and I've always meant to look at the old French lines in Africa.'

Mike's unobtrusive style contrasted with some of the videoing frenzies that went on when our train made one of its run-bys. We would stop in some picturesque spot where camcorder brigades could de-train and set up, while the engine retreated down the line before returning in a roar-past. Then it was woe betide anyone who got between gricers and their hearts' desires or, as in my case, inadvertently made some recordable aside.

Impatiently fiddling with their equipment in a corn field where a farmer and his dog looked on amazed, our videoers held their breath as engine 16194 (a Voroshilograd-built LV0062 2-10-2, if you must know) puffed itself up in a theatrical cloud of steam and smoke and charged, wailing to an Armageddon crescendo. In a cigarette-break afterglow we waited for the train to compose itself again. Petey from Ballarat was not best pleased. 'Very funny. Now it's on me tape – some drongo saying *the earth was moving for him*,' he fumed.

Mike said I was lucky to be allowed back on board.

Outside the Crimean Parliament Building in Simferopol, a heavy-weight Aussie train-spotter – with big shorts from the Rottweiler's-breakfast school of design – is too busy videoing demonstrators to notice the KGB guy in revealing 501s giving him a Ray-Ban glare that says: I'm *not* pleased to see you and this *is* a gun in my pocket.

Another undercover policeman (regulation leather jacket, Nike trainers and shades) mutters into his walkie-talkie as the trainspotter, sporting a badge that says 'Association of Railway Enthusiasts of Australia' shoves his camcorder into the face of an old woman (*babushka* headscarf, bunions erupting from what were once cheap shoes) who is waving her arms and yelling 'Nazi!' at a man carrying a Russian flag. The demo is a confusing mix of pro- and anti-government factions and Crimean separatists, and there's a lot of people in patched and musty clothes who are here presumably because they are simply fed-up with exponential inflation.

'Good on yer, Ma,' says the trainspotter, who had climbed down from the special express at Simferopol station to go in search of ice cream and got lost in the Crimean capital, pans around towards a knot of soldiers who are lounging uneasily behind a barrier. 'Mr Nasty and his banner was buggering-up my shot.'

He navigates his considerable bulk and equipment over to the front of the demo so that he can get an uninterrupted view of the parliament guards. 'I don't know what it's all about but I've got me shots,' he announces over his shoulder, not noticing that the KGB man has come over and is making vague hand motions in front of the lens. 'Hey, sport! Do you speak English?' we hear him ask, prodding the KGB man with a pudgy finger. The KGB man (amazingly) nods, but we can't see any expression through the Ray-Bans. 'Because I'd really appreciate it if you could answer me one question.' The KGB man glances over to the small group of fellow agents who are watching, alert and impassive as newts.

'Where in this whole godforsaken country,' asks the trainspotter from Yarrowee Creek, 'can I get a fair-dinkum bloody cold Pepsi?'

Sound of Lederhosen

AUSTRIA 1995

It's not the Sound of Music I'm after, hurrying south from Linz
towards a blue frieze of mountains, with the smell of alpine
meadows coming through the car's air-conditioner. Not when
I've been promised 'the inimitable thwack! of bare palms meeting
thighs covered in well-worn hide.'

Upper Austria's tourism publicists certainly know how to give
good brochure: the Thirteenth Annual Lederhosen Festival at the
little town of Windischgarsten, they say, is for 'lovers of leather'
and comes complete with 'ancient fertility rites' and 'rumbustious
celebrations.' I can't wait.

We cross the wavy edge of the Salzkammergut – a wide,
pre-Alpen landscape of glacier-carved valleys an hour's drive east
from Salzburg – a continuing favourite venue (despite a too-strong
Schilling) with British walkers. The Wolfgangsee, Mondsee, Attersee
and the Traunsee – huge lakes – were 'discovered' in the last century
by the resorting bourgeoisie of Vienna and Salzburg, and many
towns roundabout still have an air of strait-laced, *fin de siècle* fun:
water-cures, heavy dinners and light music... a touch of the Mario
Lanzas. You wouldn't be surprised, almost, to see a roly-poly tenor

in tights and bright orange slap turning St Wolfgang's ritzy-historic lake-front into the set for an operetta. The White Horse Inn, it's claimed, is the very hostelry that inspired and gave a name to that classic Thirties musical.

Franz Lehar and the last-but-one Habsburg emperor, Franz Joseph, spent their summers at nearby Bad Ischl: Lehar in the Leharvilla, composing melodies for *The Merry Widow*, *Land of Smiles* and the like, surrounded by his amazing collection of religiose/erotic pictures; the Kaiser in the Kaiservilla, signing the odd Declaration of War, watched over (reproachfully, presumably) by the stuffed heads of his multitudinous hunting victims.

'It's a weird place, Austria,' I hear myself saying as we roll at last into the banner-flapped streets of Windischgarsten. 'Oh, but we have the home-loving natures,' says Judith, the young Tourist Officer, performing a masterful parking manoeuvre. 'For us everything must be very much *gemütlich*.' I wind the window down and listen out for thwacks.

They're not long in coming: a British Press photographer has dragooned a couple of burly local men in leather shorts into a brief bout of leg-cuffing in front of the bandstand. 'I only came for the thigh-slapping stuff,' he confides to me. I have to admit to doubts that such pantomime thwackery could be regarded as authentic – unlike (I hasten to add) his own admirable, 24-carat chutzpah. 'Image is all,' he says, snapping away.

Windischgarsten, according to my 1929 Baedeker, is a prettily situated market-village which makes a good base, at around 2,000 feet, for walks and climbs. The 7,828-foot Warscheneck climb, it says, should take seven hours and is 'not difficult'. Strolls to the scythe factory and to the Ursprungstein Grotto – a deep, blue pool from which issues the infant Piessling River – are recommended. Scythe factory or not, Karl Baedeker would certainly recognise the place, although he might be taken aback to see today's line-up for the Miss Lederhosen Contest.

'It's revolution idea: women with lederhosen,' admits Gerald Reindl of the Leonding Lederhosen Club, recovering over his litre of beer at the bar after a celebratory polka around the Town Square with the contest winner, fellow club member Silvia Stiegler. 'In olden times, women with lederhosen was not normal here,' says Gerald, an office worker from near Linz. 'Normal for them was dirndls and fashion clothes.' 'Pfui!' comments the new Miss Lederhosen.

Gerald uses the word 'normal' in the sense of 'accepted'. And it soon becomes clear, as we talk over some more glasses of beer, that the wearing of lederhosen, by either sex, has not always been as acceptable as it was in Baedeker's time and as it is now. From the end of the War until the '80s, the wearing of Austria's (and many other countries') national dress was often regarded as, at least, a sign of chauvinism; today, lederhosen are politically comfortable. 'For years we didn't wear it,' says Gerald. 'And then a few years ago some friends were starting to do this and I thought "why not?", and so I have now this wonderful experience of the leather shorts…which, by the way, are very expensive!'

Not just the shorts. At Franz Tschitscho's stall down the road, goat-hide lederhosen are walking away at £225 the pair, but a full man's rig requires special hand-made shoes *Goiserer*, made in the village of Bad Goisern, which cost at least £300, and a hat-ornament made from chamois neck-hairs – a *Gamsbart* – which alone will set you back a cool thousand or so quid.

'It means climbing very high to hunt the Gemser,' explains Gerald, as I nearly drop my beer on the cobbles in alarm at the hat-decoration price-tag. 'I don't know…maybe as high as where grows the edelweiss.' 'Higher than,' says Miss Lederhosen, firmly. We lift our glasses and toast the nimble chamois and its home, the not-so-distant, lavender-coloured mountains. Oompah music drifts our way from the direction of Windischgarsten's pedestrian zone. We watch children converge wolfishly for the unveiling of a 'Lederhosencake' big enough to envelop a snooker table. There is a squeal from above.

A roped-on tot in alpine costume has just completed a 'rock climb' – a five storey-high studded wooden wall – from which height, like a frustrated eaglet he contemplates the cake demolition below.

But thigh-slapping calls. Saying goodbye to Miss Lederhosen and Gerald, and giving a cheery wave to the cakeless mountaineer, I head through a leathered throng (and, I realise, a Kaiser's ransom in chamois tufts) towards the sound of yodelling. Where there's yodelling, I reckon, thigh-slapping cannot be far away.

I find that I have joined a well-oiled Chapter of Austrian Hell's Angels who are watching a sort of karaoke version of Sumo wrestling and listening to Tex Robinson's Country Music combo. In short order I am invited to (a) don a sweat-box Michelin Man safety costume and wrestle the 'Hallstatt Hippo' for a purse of 1,000 schillings, and (b) waltz to Tex's version of *Stand by Your Man* with a large biker girl and her Megadeath T-shirt. I explain to the Hippo and to Mitzi Megadeath that my particular devotion right now has to be to yodelling and the punishment of leather-covered thighs. This info seems to get me quite a lot of respect. More and stranger invitations are coming my way. I have to make my excuses and leave. (Where, I wonder, is my protector and guide, Judith?)

'Blown it, mate – I'm gutted,' says a lugubrious voice in my ear. The photographer has just missed snapping the one brief but authentic thigh-slapping dance of the day. 'I did get the winner of the Furthest Travelled Lederhosen event. Perfect: nine months old and all the way from Pakistan. Good light. Now I discover he's called Adrian Godfrey...which just won't look right in a caption. Why couldn't he be a Jürgen or a Fritz?'

After considering and then abandoning the idea of seeking out a local farmer called Polz who, it seems, has carried off the prize for Most Creative Lederhosen ('I've got too many farmers already,' says my friend) we chill out with a beer and sausage over by the old-fashioned brass band.

I buy a gingerbread heart (*Lebkuchenherz*) with 'Dearest One' written in swirly icing sugar. It's an appropriate talisman for my next project: checking out the Kiosks of Kitsch. These little temporary wooden booths are blamelessly spick and span, each one as lovingly rusticated as a cuckoo clock. They are trying to tell me – as well as sell me – something. What is the sub-text of, for instance: name-swags of flounced ribbon saying things like 'Mummy's Kitchen,' 'Daddy's Den,' 'The Most Important Room?' Teams of sinister, benzedrine-eyed moppet dolls and flights of warty witches? Surreal profusions of (from the My Little Pony school of aesthetics) embroidered place-settings and wickery, ribbony hanging things? Troves of lacily nubile scatter-cushions?

In the absence of a style-guru to talk me through that lot, I ask Mrs Hartl – stallholder, and every inch the demure *hausfrau* in her dirndl and embroidered blouse – which objects she thinks most embody Upper Austrian *Weltanschauung*. 'Of course, the pillows are very important,' she replies, picking up an elaborate, pastel-pink number from her Zierpolster stock. 'And we always give them this little Karate-chop on top so that they sit properly...like this.' We both admire her newly plumped cushion with its symmetrical crease. Because, adds Mrs Hartl with a conspiratorial wink, '*Ordnung muss sein*' – there must be order.

New Heart of Germany

'They're not very obvious, don't you think?' law student Axel says, turning his left profile so that I can see the thin, pale, tell-tale lines on his 23-year-old brow. He is showing me his sabre scars.

Axel's are the healed tracks of razor-sharp cuts received in the *Mensur* – the bloody rite-of-passage practised by élite fraternities for more than 200 years that now, controversially, is regaining popularity at some older German universities.

Through a scented canopy of lime-flowers and orange-blossom in the garden of this rather grand house on Rottendorfer Strasse, which is the headquarters of the 175-year-old Bavaria Fencing Corps, sunlight slices prettily across our glasses of beer. Just below are the spires of the old university city of Würzburg, and across the valley of the River Main neatly incised vineyards slope up to the medieval walls of Castle Marienberg. This used to be Cold War territory, a short tank rumble from what was the western edge of the Soviet Empire; now the heart of a bustling, confident new Germany.

The young men here in the garden, with their discreet facial scars above light blue, dark blue and white fraternity ribbands, are enjoying a Saturday lunchtime break from their books. Axel and his friends are in the midst of exams. Around the barbecue, conversations are subdued. The Corps' bunker-sized beer store beneath the fraternity house is not getting many customers.

After reading tabloid accounts of Corps' activities and hearing a few breathless denunciations from worried Germans, I'd arrived half expecting to find myself in an eagle's nest of heel-clicking *Jugend*. At the very least, I had thought, these sabre-wielding students, whose supposed activities and attitudes make them anathema to so many modern Germans, would have their PR guards well up. Instead, here am I being welcomed with beer, beefsteak and potato salad – and as far as I could tell, not a Hooray Heinrich in sight.

'Great fear in my guts, I was very, very afraid. In a sort of dream. All I could hear was my heart. I thought "please don't let me faint." Then, when I felt a blade whistling past my head, I started to feel OK. When I saw blood streaming down, I was suddenly filled with joy. It was my blood.' Other Corps members around our table nod solemnly at Axel describing his first *Mensur*.

Würzburg has 13 fencing fraternities, and there are thought to be about 3,000 '*actives*' – sabre-fencing students – in Germany. *Alte Herren*, 'Old Boys' who continue to contribute money and support to their student organisations throughout their lives after leaving university, number perhaps another 20,000. Every would-be member must prove himself in – usually two – 'sharp' engagements against rival Corps members before he can wear the three-coloured fraternity sash.

In Würzburg's Bavaria Corps, full members are expected to complete five more *Parties*: the traditional *Mensur* encounter consisting of 120 strikes of the *Corpsschläger*. Outsiders are not allowed to see these events, which bear little relation to what is more generally understood by the word 'fencing'. Standing rigidly four-square to each other a blade's length apart, swaddled in chainmail and thick leather, and wearing heavy gauntlets and iron goggles, Corps participants twirl their 90cm-long lovingly sharpened blades, Magi-Mix fashion. There is no scoring of points –

only the shared giving and receiving of the required 120 sabre passes that comprise one *Mensur*. Bouts are stopped if a participant receives a bad cut. Stepping back or flinching away from an opponent can earn shameful disqualification – although how the referees can tell (cringe detectors?) what's going on inside all that metal and leather beats me. A sabre's point is squared off 'so that it stops at the bone and won't slide under the skin'. I squirm (maybe I even flinch) at the word 'bone' but my Bavaria Corps hosts are much too polite to notice.

Mensuren are formal and, like many other fraternity activities – including beer sessions – subject to rigid codes of behaviour called *Comment*. The terms used by fencing fraternities are a reminder that the German tradition has roots in the deadly fad for duelling of post-Revolution France.

'We are not barbarians, I think,' ventures Thomas, Bavaria Corps' 27-year-old spokesman, veteran of eight *Mensuren*, who will soon be taking his economics and resources management degrees out into the world of corporate marketing. 'We wear so much protection that we have only a possibility of taking clean, straight cuts to the temple. Not so dangerous, I think, as your rugby football.'

Thomas just has time to add that the *Mensur* 'is a ritual by which we can learn to experience and overcome fear' before he is summoned away to the phone to be torn off a strip by his girlfriend. She wants to know why the entertainment of some foreign reporter is more important than their date.

'What do girls think about scars?' André, a visitor wearing the blue/white/orange colours of Würzburg's 1836 Nassovia Corps, who appears unmarked after six *Mensuren*, lifts aside a lock of hair so that I can just make out his three ghostly lines. 'You know, some girls they don't like them at all…but others, well, *they really like them*.'

The *Mensur* as it stands today (a somewhat chastened Thomas reveals as we look around the Corps headquarters) bears little relation to the hyper-sanguinary and often fatal student rituals of the late 19th and early 20th centuries.

The fencing room, with its old-fashioned high windows, chalky paint and iron radiators, is more Sunday School than Grand Guignol – even with those racks of chilling, basket-handled sabres. There isn't any blood on the floor.

'We wouldn't expect a Corps man to accept any anaesthetic for the sewing-up,' says Thomas nonchalantly, in the medical room: stainless-steel sterilising unit and (I can't help noticing) cheek-high operating lights. Doctors attending *Mensuren* are usually Old Boys. 'But we are not into that old macho blood and iron business where a big scar – a *Millionenmarkschmiss* they called it – was more important to career prospects than a good degree.' No. The thing today is *Verbindung*: 'a binding together based on keeping one's word, reliability...,' explains Thomas before (no doubt biting his tongue) being abruptly summoned away to meet she-of-the-phone-call who has now appeared in person to give him a piece of her mind.

'We're not popular right now – she's quite annoyed,' mutters a newly scarred recruit glancing furtively towards the front of the Corps house. I keep a low profile behind my beer and contemplate distant vineyards flanking the Main, reminded that the flowery white Franconian wine produced here and the local beer are as deservedly famous as each other. Which is as serendipitous a state of affairs as anyone could wish for. The Main is a link between the Danube and the Rhine, meandering through gentle countryside, reflecting Gothic and Baroque spires and tying together (*Verbindung* again) equally strong Catholic and Protestant traditions along the way.

Würzburg itself, once one of Germany's most important episcopal cities, and one which lost most of its architectural heritage during one Allied bombing raid in 1945, is contentedly, sleepily reconciled to its new fame as the starting point for tourists doing the Romantic Road through Bavarian Swabia to the Allgäu.

Bamberg, 60 or so kilometres upriver, gives a good idea of what the historic centre of Würzburg must have been like: it's one of the best-preserved small towns in Germany and an unmissable destination for any serious student of architecture (everything from

Romanesque onwards) or beer (nine breweries making 49 different beers in the town and 100-plus breweries in the immediate countryside around).

'We tend not to lay too much stress on the fact this area is the beer centre of the world,' Anna-Maria Schülein from the Bamberg Tourist Office had admitted. 'Some people think that isn't very serious.' We had ducked off the cobbles of Dominikanerstrasse into the 17th-century tavern Schlenkerla for state-of-the-art *Rauchbier* (a heady dark brew from smoke-dried malt) accompanied by some definitive roasted local sausage – quite serious enough for me.

It has to be admitted that Bamberg has other goodies: the paintings of Lucas Cranach the Elder in the Staatsgalerie at the overwhelmingly Baroque Neue Residenz palace, for starters. And in the Romanesque cathedral reside exquisite (look at the way the hands of the figures are delineated) early 16th-century stone friezes by Tilman Riemenschneider. Here is the strange and wonderful *Bamberg Rider* equestrian statue – probably of a Hungarian king, although nobody knows for sure.

Like Wagner's music (and Bayreuth is just down the road, though it might as well be in Valhalla as far as your chances of obtaining tickets to the *Ring* are concerned) this work of art has to live under the shadow of Hitler's ludicrous enthusiasm. The Schicklgruber Effect. Which might be the case with the *Mensur*. Just as the Führer saw in the *Bamberg Rider* the very embodiment of Germanic warrior perfection, he regarded the *Mensur* – which when he became Chancellor in 1933 had been technically illegal for 50 years – with a beady, proprietorial eye. Formal legality was imposed upon the Corps, along with racial 'purification'.

When Jewish students were banned in 1933, says Thomas, 30 Old Boys of Bavaria Corps – who happened to be non-Jews – left in protest. 'In our archives we have their sad letters of resignation, and ones from the Jewish student members at that time who left rather than see the Corps punished. Quite a lot of Corps simply disbanded themselves.'

Mensur is seen as being anything from pointlessly old-fashioned to gung-ho atavistic by a majority of German students: an attempt was made to burn down a Corps house at Göttingen, and members have been shot at in the ex-East German town of Halle. Thomas readily admits that not all fraternities are like Bavaria Corps, 'some only accept German nationals who have completed military service – the sort of clubs that tend to sing 'Deutschland, Deutschland über alles' at their social evenings. In Bavaria Corps we are true to our pro-democracy, open-to-all beginnings in 1820. And these days we have great discos. We bop.'

Thomas gives me a lift to Würzburg railway station. He hopes I'm not going to write a scare story. Coming from a country of Sieg Heil-ing Barmy Army sports fans, who am I to point the finger of political correctness? Compared with the beer-bombastic (and much-scarred) rugger club types of my acquaintance, I tell him, Corps men are models of civilised behaviour.

They might not be exactly representative of modern Germany, but neither do Corps men shape up as dangerous reincarnations of the old blood and honour elite – any more than do the tattooed and much-pierced punk youngsters who presently are kind enough to show me the way to the ticket office.

The Samosa's Revenge

GUJARAT 1995

Jolted awake as the narrow-gauge train creeps excruciatingly up to buffers. Diesel fume and dust, and a turbanned face at the open window saying: 'Coolie, Sah'b?' This is Bhuj, the capital of Kutch, Gujarat's north-western extremity at the top left-hand corner of India. And it's the end of the line.

'Don't be so feeble!' hisses Bettina, the India expert. I languish sweatily (I'm not feeling very well) over our baggage on the hot station concrete and she strides off to bully one of the clamouring tuk-tuk drivers into carrying us downtown for no more than two or three times the local rate. Perched wanly on our luggage in the back of the tiny three-wheeler as we dodge the usual ruck of Kamikaze drivers and supercilious cows, I'm wondering which of my two days' worth of railway snacks since leaving Delhi was the culprit. 'What do you mean "It could be serious this time?" You've just got a little tummy-bug because you're too cowardly to complain when someone sells you a yesterday's samosa!' says my travelling companion. She's one of those irritating people who are never ill.

Nice Mr Vinod Gor of the sympathetic brown eyes, however,

knows an invalid when he sees one. The equally smiling Gor brothers run the basic, old-fashioned hotel and restaurant, the Annapurna, next to one of the ancient – still bristling with elephant-spikes – city gates. 'You need rest,' divines Mr Vinod at once, 'and some special Indian medicine which I will be arranging.' Just the job. Suddenly, I don't mind not having television or air-conditioning. Fate and the tuk-tuk man having brought us to the Annapurna (Bettina is looking doubtful) we might as well go with the flow, I reckon. It's a karmic matter. TV and AC, I plead, are not so important as TLC.

This is a great way to trail-blaze: dozing and reading under a fan at the Annapurna, while Bettina battles the glare and dust of this rarely visited city and returns with reports. Mr Vinod brings me regular doses of his Ayurvedic cure-all – a not untasty porridge of fleaseed husks – and congratulates me on being a 'real' traveller, saying I'm one of the very few foreign visitors who ever make it as far as Bhuj. The shuttered room is soothing. I don't think I'll risk going outside just yet.

Bhuj has one of the oldest (1877) museums in India – one of those wonderful Victorian rag-bag collections of everything: bullet-dented armour and the wonky stuffed heads of unlucky beasts who once made someone's day. There are exquisite miniature paintings and now unrecognisable vegetable and animal curiosities in formaldehyde. After raving about the museum's collection of textiles, Bettina discovers that genuine old stuff can be found in the bazaar – *bandhani* tie and dye for which this area is famous, *shisha* embroidery with sewn-on tiny mirrors and *katab*, the traditional appliqué work of Kutchi herders. She hits the shopping button. The room becomes a repository for piles of ancient Gujarati embroideries and mirror-work – and for a carved wooden parrot (of the kind that can still be seen over the doors of Bhuj's older houses), several wooden bowls, a massive tribal necklace of woven silver – together with (and I think this is going too far luggage-wise) a collection of Bohemian glass oil lamps. 'They've been in India for 100 years or more – now we will take them back to Europe,' says

Bettina complacently, going off to buy a tin trunk. I don't like the sound of that 'we'.

It seems Bhuj has a dilapidated Maharaja's palace and a lake lined with many falling-down temples and burning ghats. Vicariously, I mingle with peasant and pastoral castes (Rabari, Ahir and Kanbe), in their timeless traditional clothes, thronging the narrow streets inside the city walls. 'And you'll be glad to know that tomorrow you'll be up and about and able to look at things for yourself,' adds Bettina firmly, showing me a permit from the Bhuj military police office to visit the Rann of Kutch. The Rann is a semi-wilderness bordering Pakistan, created 100 or so years ago by a shift in the course of the River Indus. 'And for goodness' sake,' she adds, 'go down to the bazaar and get a shave.'

You don't just get a shave: it's a hot towels, twice over with the cutthroat, rose-water and talc job. For 20p. Mr Sami the barber sends me out into the world with a new baby's bottom face, which continues to tingle hours later on the clapped-out bus heading along overgrown tracks into the Rann. Thorn bushes whip at us through open windows. Smiling golden smiles, the other passengers cover their heads with colourful scarves against incoming dust. I am dying for a cup of tea.

We are ushered off in what looks like the middle of nowhere and stand with our suitcases on hot sand under a withering sun. The driver grinds gears and shouts 'Have nice day!' and goes off in a cloud. Far ahead on one side stretch the parched territories of Sind and the Thar Desert; to the other, nothing but salt-flats for 100 miles or so until the Arabian Sea. I'm about to mutter something along the lines of 'another fine mess you've got me into' when two barefoot boys materialise from behind the thorn bushes and march off with our luggage. Naturally, we trudge through the scrub in the general direction they seem to have taken, suddenly emerging onto a narrow lane of dried buffalo dung beside neat, two-room huts. A woman with a gold nostril ring, in a brightly coloured skirt and mirror-embroidered bodice, stares in surprise and then snatches a wide-eyed child back through a doorway. Further on there is a larger hut where I catch sight of our baggage just inside the open door. I'm about to reach in when, out of the gloom, a hand grasps mine and shakes it warmly. 'Welcome to Hodaka,' says a large man dressed in western slacks and shirt. 'You look as if you could do with a cup of tea, isn't it?'

Mr Basar Bhura is headman of the village and has just returned from trade-fairs in Germany and Japan. One-camel-two-television Hodaka, a typical Rann settlement of 'low' caste Meghwal leather workers – many of whom seldom venture even as far as Bhuj – has become an important test village for government plans to nurture handicraft industries.

At the threshold of the community hut where we sit drinking delicious tea, the headman's terminally dusty winklepickers are parked next to a pair of smart Bombay slip-ons. Mr Basar Bhura is negotiating a pile of goods with a man wearing the obligatory massive gold watch of the merchant. The embroidery of the women of Hodaka these days finds a ready market, but it seems to me that the work now being churned out for cash is not comparable with the wonderful old handcraft that is still in everyday use. The well-worn old *ralli* – an appliquéd and embroidered bed quilt glowing with fragments of old print and *mashru* – that a village woman is using to carry her stock of new embroidery costs £8. She thinks I'm mad.

Despite exposure at international trade fairs and the visits of Bombay shopkeepers, Hodaka is still remote enough to have preserved old ideas of hospitality. There are invitations to enter family huts, to sit on quilts, to drink more sweet tea ('The more sugar we give, the more we love you!'). Interiors are simple and elegant, with utensils stowed away on ledges and roof beams, and the centre piece and source of much pride is the elaborate shrine-cum-cupboard of painted and mirrored dried mud. In the evening, Mr Basar Bhura fires up his generator and invites us into his family hut for dinner: *kidjeri* – a mess of coarse rice and mung beans in buffalo milk – followed by onion curry, chapattis and buttermilk. We chew betel nut and the headman's brother hands round a brass pot of ground antimony to line our eyelids. This is thought to be very beneficial for sight. Bettina says I look like Betty Boop.

Under quilts on frame beds outside the guest hut, we fall asleep listening to a dogs' chorus and counting stars and meteorites. At dawn, the sun is a lemon ball on the horizon and women walk by with brass water pots. Cows and buffalo are coming in from the scrublands. A boy brings a can of water and leads me off to the ablutions area. He is nonplussed when I make a bee-line for the distant clump of bushes where I want to sniff some custard-coloured trumpet flowers. I have seen them before, from trains, and have wondered for hundreds of miles what they smell like. It's perfect vanilla, with something meaty prowling around in the background – definitely one for the smell collection.

It's time to move on – before Bettina buys any more stuff – and I'm secretly relieved that our train arrangements for travelling south don't allow any stop-off time in Gujarat's largest city, Ahmadabad. The city has some of India's finest Mughal architecture, but it's also famous for textiles (Ahmadabad is 'the Manchester of India') and jewellery as well as heavy and awkward-to-carry copper and brass vessels, lacquer boxes and stone and wood carvings. I suspect that there would be quite a lot of Bohemian glass lamps still knocking about, too. Instead, our first stop is Surat, centre of textile dyeing and gold and silver thread manufacture, and once the most important port of the Mughal empire. 'And just the place for a hypochondriac,' says Bettina, reminding me that Surat's all-too-recent fame was on account of an outbreak of pneumonic plague. A double room at Hotel Dreamland costs 50p – not bad, even if the old bakelite TV smokes slightly and smells like hot dog breath.

'Hooray! Hot water!' cries my friend from the bathroom – then 'Boo! No cold water!' There's always something.

Our carefully rationed duty-free Scotch has run out and I've been looking forward to Daman, which we reach after a short, crowded excursion on a branch line to Vapi followed by a 20p taxi ride. Along with Diu, its twin sister port higher up the coast on the opposite side of the Gulf of Khambhat, Daman is a tiny oasis of alcohol in an otherwise dry state. Portugal's 450-year rule came to an abrupt end in 1961 with the Indian Army take-over, but Iberian images still catch the eye: a barefoot, gypsy-like woman in flounced dress and high shouldered blouse, a bungalow called 'Casa Oriental', the baroque, twisted barley sugar columns of a 17th-century chapel – and the bars. With its silted-up harbour under the ancient fort on the Ganga River and its air of submerging colonialism, it smells of drying fish – and its rows of beer and spirit joints – Daman is reincarnated as a weekend resort for boozers.

Lots of cheap drink about (hooray!) but I can't have any (boo!) because I'm suffering the effects of another duff samosa. It's mineral water for me, and resting in the room with the alarming mountain of shopping. Bettina (for once) is sympathetic: 'You relax while I do the markets – this looks like a good place to find more old oil lamps.'

Prince Pickle and the
Heavenly Cucumbers

EAST GERMANY 1996

I have seen the future and it seems to be covered with graffiti...
I find myself whingeing to no one in particular as I gawp out of a bus
window at the ever-growing building site that is Berlin. I just have
time to clock that the *Zeitgeist* on both sides of the city's old east/west
divide now wields the same spray can, wears the same hard hat, is
glued to the same car phone at the same traffic lights and is demanding
the same spare change while slumped in the same doorway...
before I catch a train back to the 1950s.

The immaculate Deutsche Bahn train hurries from Bahnhof
Lichtenberg and plunges out of tattooed suburbia before heading
south and east into the lowlands of the River Spree. Soon we are
deep in what was once the heart of the GDR – now big Germany's
easternmost border.

A funky change from the rather overdone orderliness and
prosperity further west, it is a landscape where women in headscarves
bend over vegetable plots. The smokeless chimney of a down-at-heel
factory goes by, and a mangy Trabi (these cheeky little everlasting
Eastern Bloc runabouts should come with nicotine stained two-finger

badges on the bonnet) waits like an old dog outside a home-made bungalow. I am tempted to get off at one of the little village stations with their cobbles, gaslights and pre-War lettering just to see if I really have arrived in another time dimension.

This is shed territory. A comforting, allotment quality suffuses dinky fields of maize (how often do you see a small field of anything these days?) and lends a modest romance to scabby industrial units beside the track. It's a golden enough post-Soviet afternoon, and even the occasional proletarian high-rise doesn't spoil the *déjà-vu*.

I'm going to Cottbus (where? I hear you cry). Cottbus is 70-odd miles from Berlin and was in the last century one of Brandenburg's foremost cities, growing richly baroque from its textile mills and surrounding brown-coal mines. Now, after sell-off and the advance of eco-law, it is much reduced. Western funds are cleaning Cottbus' 19th-century bourgeois façades, but they are not replacing the industry that was responsible for both the grime and all that splendid stonework.

So why go there? Well, ravages of war, communism and market force permitting, I am hoping to find one of the wonders of late 19th-century Europe: the English garden of Prince Hermann von Pückler-Muskau (of whom more, later). And the area just happens to be the pickled cucumber capital of the universe.

Let us bow to historical priority, and the fact that for many visitors they are anyway the main draw, and consider first the Cucurbitaceae. To do this we will have to get down from our lovely train six miles short of Cottbus at the picturesque town of Lübbenau where the station seems to have changed little since it opened for business in 1866. And the sign gives an alternative version, Lubnjow, of the town's name, a reminder that this area – 600 miles of waterways of the upper Spree winding and doubling back through woods, fields, market gardens and villages – is the traditional home of the westernmost Slavs, the Sorbs.

A boggy wilderness, the area was the Sorbs' exclusive domain until the coming of the Berlin, Cottbus, Görlitz railway. Then the area –

the Spreewald – became a favourite weekending destination for Berliners. And the word was out: those Sorbs know a thing or two about pickled cucumber…and boiled carp…and smoked eel.

'Yes, some people are too interested in only the food of the Sorbenland,' says Ms Kilka the tourist guide. 'We feel sorry for them, because they miss the best thing which is the history and the culture.' The exquisite reek of dill is too much for me. Helplessly, I reach for yet another taste torpedo from my presentation pack of cucumbers in garlic brine. They, and the punt in which we are now threading reed-thronged willowy canals, are courtesy of the Lübbenau Tourism Board.

In the manner of the nuclear submarines which they resemble in miniature, Spreewalder Gurken nudge their way to the surface through spicy flotsam to deliver pre-emptive strikes on unsuspecting taste buds. Then, as I try to point out to my boating companions, it's goodbye piccalilli, farewell effete little cocktail party gherkins on sticks. 'Hmm,' says Ms Kilka doubtfully.

The Sorb population, even with migrant communities in Australia, South Africa and the USA, has gone down from 200,000 to about 67,000 in the last 100 years. During the 1930s, top Nazis wanted to clear dozens of villages and turn the Spreewald into a private hunting park. The government now provides guarantees and support for Sorb culture, but the language, related to but distinct from both Polish and Czech, is these days not much heard outside of the classroom or the folk fest.

Our boatman poles us between overgrown banks and fields of horseradish to the village of Lehde. At water cross roads, signs point the way to waterland villages, many of which are only accessible by boat, although the area now has an extensive cycle and hiking network making use of small, hump-backed bridges. Just about all the 2.8 million annual visitors to the Spreewald are from eastern Germany and Poland, with a tiny percentage from Scandinavia.

Spreewald postmen punt their way around in summer and ice skate in winter. The area suffered from power station effluent during the Communist era but is now a UNESCO Biosphere Reserve and the home of otters, cranes, storks, eagles and many other rare species. Animals that had almost disappeared during the bad old days of pollution are now increasing. 'Like the Sorb culture, they never quite died out completely,' says Ms Kilka.

Spree water, as our boatman demonstrates, is drinkable again – a fact of enormous local significance. Sorb girls carried on their tradition of enhancing beauty and marriage-luck by secret bathing on Easter night despite dead fish.

I take another hit of the Tourist Board's gift of herb intensive Spreewald liqueur (imagine hair conditioner with attitude and you get the idea) and enquire about the massive old barrels beside the landing-stages. 'Superseded pickle technology,' explains Ms Kilka. Seeing my eyebrows begin to elevate themselves, she adds, 'yes, five tons at one time of pickled cucumbers.' Then, disposing of this non-subject once and for all 'and if they leaked into the river that was very bad news for the crayfishes.'

It doesn't bear thinking about what would have happened to local morale if the old pickle industry and the brown-coal power station between them had managed to do in the last crayfish. The creatures are a Cottbus leitmotif. Ms Scholz, from the city's Tourism Office, points them out on medieval coats of arms in the Oberkirche of St Nikolas, on old iron door knockers around town and incised on stone over doorways. In the Oberkirche, stuffed behind a wooden cross, we find a couple of post-atheism scribbled votive messages: 'I don't believe in God but help me get my kids Nicole and Doreen back,' and 'Thank God for a boyfriend.'

Cottbus was food famous long before it became cloth and lignite rich. Maybe delicatessen is coming back into the frame. At any rate, the new municipal stone monument at the Altmarkt fountain commemorates not only (wouldn't you know it?) those heavenly cucumbers but also the carp farmers of nearby Peitz and one Maria Groch, inventor of *Baumkuchen* cake in the form of a tree trunk (they laughed at Sacher and his Torte, remember?).

Ms Scholz and I set off walking from the crane-dominated city centre (Cottbus is building and renovating, and finding lots of unexploded World War 2 bombs, just like Berlin) through the ring of redundant textile mills (now serving as car parks where the glossiest Mercedes and BMWs keep company with tough little Moskvichs and Trabis) to Prince Hermann von Pückler-Muskau's domain in the leafy suburb of Branitz. We cross a road and take a small path through woods that open out into what looks like classic English parkland. Surrounded by an artfully meandering stream and a lake is a perfect mini mansion.

This estate took 25 years, up to the Prince's death in 1871, to create. The last and greatest 19th-century German landscape garden, it has taken until now to reach maturity. Prince Hermann's vision of incorporating rare trees from all over the world with native varieties in a deceptively natural setting that could evolve with the seasons, can now be seen in its full glory.

We cross rivulets of the Spree via Prussian-blue cast-iron bridges, skirt a lake from which a huge grown-over earth pyramid arises, keeping company with another pyramid on the garden side, and arrive at the Schloss by way of an iron and gilt rose arbour. We ascend stone steps and pay a few marks to go in by the beautiful blue front door. Original portraits, sketches, *objets d'art*, furniture, as well as the well-kept-up gardens around, add to the impression that the noble family are still at home – although like other landowners in East Germany they fled when their possessions were seized at the end of the War.

'It will not be fair,' cries Ms Scholz suddenly, 'if the family now come from the West and take it all back and we, who looked after it all the years, can no longer come.' It's a heartfelt little outburst that these days finds many echoes throughout the old GDR.

In his own time, the prince actually encouraged the lower orders to walk around his grounds as long as they refrained from canoodling or wearing high heels. His own behaviour, on the other hand, was probably par for the 19th-century aristocratic course: no high heels, it seems, but he did come back from a grand tour with an Ethiopian slave girl, and he did race a carriage drawn by a team of stags along Berlin's Kurfürstendamm. He gardened with Prussian thoroughness and even found time to write a series of travel memoirs and textbooks on garden layout and architecture, one of which remains a standard text.

So grandiose was Prince Hermann's landscaping for the family lands at Muskau (bestriding the nearby Polish border and now sadly derelict) that he avoided bankruptcy only by selling-up and moving to the much smaller estate at Branitz, having first tried to score a rich bride from among the upwardly straining industrialists' daughters of England. Before setting out on this quest, he even, with much mutual anguish, obtained a divorce of convenience from his ever-devoted wife Lucie, a touch prematurely, it turned out, because the prince's fortune-hunt fizzled when Charles Dickens got up a moral crusade in the Press of the day. The prince was accused of everything from lounge-lizardry to double-parking the stags. After the final indignity of being parodied as 'Prince Pickle' (could this be a subconscious Dickensian reference to Spreewald cucumbers?) poor Hermann escaped back to Lucie and to Branitz.

All this is pretty unlikely material, you might think, to make good, old-fashioned romance, but standing on one of Hermann's Prussian-blue bridges in the midst of his lovely park, and with the Pückler-Muskau schloss outlining the companion pyramids (His'n'Hers?), where the Prince and Lucie are now buried, it really is the only word that will do.

Coromandel Coast

INDIA 1996

We feel like truants out of school, sitting on Pondicherry's old colonial sea-front eating cardamom-scented ice creams and watching tigerish rollers coming in from the Bay of Bengal. Bettina and I are discovering that, after the rigours of being on the road in south India, France's ex-colony on the Coromandel Coast is a great place to chill out.

For sheer religion inducing terror, it's hard to beat driving or being driven along the trunk roads of India. Our hire car drivers on this trip have, true to form, made it a point of honour to overtake on blind corners and charge – with horn accompaniment – all oncoming lorries. All complaints from the back seat are referred, with pious smirks, to the omnipresent glow-in-the-dark Vishnu on the dashboard. We arrived in Pondy grateful that karma has saved us to cringe another day.

For the time being, blissfully, there's nothing to do. It's fine by me that Pondicherry appears not to have any noteworthy temples or famous artisan markets or that the town museum seems permanently closed for repairs. What – I want to know as we stroll through the little town where bougainvillea overgrows ice cream coloured colonial walls and Tamil gendarmes in red *kepis* whistle ineffectually at the traffic – could be more heavenly than chancing upon a south Indian town with cheese sandwiches, cold beer and reasonably recent European newspapers?

'Whose side are you on?' the youth who hangs out at the corner of Lal Bahadur Shastri Street and Rue Dumas wants to know. Is there after all something serpent-like in this well supplied and laid back Garden of Eden? Narayanan, who prefers to be known as Elvis and claims to be a punk, wears bogus Ray-Bans and a Sex Pistols T-shirt with a modest rip. Elvis tells me that foreigners arriving in Pondy have to be Ashramites or Aurovilians. 'No fence-sitting here, man,' he admonishes.

'Aspire to the Divine' posters and the rather disconcerting gaze of Pondy's two famous spiritual leaders are displayed in shops, travel agents, government offices and even bars. The political exile and teacher who came to be known as Sri Aurobindo founded an ashram here in 1926 and his French partner, known as The Mother, carried on the work after Aurobindo's death and also started a new-age community, Auroville, just outside the town. Followers of two gurus, many of whom are westerners, dominate the area's political and commercial life. For reasons no one, not even Elvis, seems able to explain, relations between the two groups fell into disharmony. Fatwas abounded. Pondicherry was invisibly divided. Elvis and I, in our daily conversations, quickly exhaust the topic of guru wars and get on to *Star Wars,* of which film he has an encyclopaedic knowledge. And Elvis kindly undertakes to educate me in the arcana of punk rock. After each tutorial I stroll from 'Blacktown' west of the canal into 'Whitetown' (both colonial terms still used by locals) in search of an English newspaper and a large bottle of Haywards Export straight out of the fridge at the Seagull Restaurant. I usually have curried prawns and sit on the veranda to watch Tamil fishermen sneak through the surf on the lashed-together logs of their catamarans. For me, this is about as divine as things get.

I like Pondy's turn-of-the-century seafront with its restful, post-colonial scruffiness and statue of Governor General Dupleix, mastermind of the single French victory, in 1748, over the British. This was one of a series of imperial spats that resulted in the colony changing its flag four times. Was there somewhere to go after Pondy? Elvis had heard of an old port, just south of the Cauvery River delta, where aliens (in the form of 17th-century Danish adventurers) built a fort.

Gold coins litter the beach, he claims. The place is called Tharangambadi, 'the place where the waves sing' in Tamil. Just the job, I say. Elvis thinks I might like to give him an agent's commission in respect of any gold I find on the beach but settles for the promise of a postcard. He waves goodbye saying, 'may The Force go with you!' The Force, in the person of Bettina, has already made all the arrangements. Shamelessly, she has beaten down the hire price for a tidy old Ambassador to £10 a day. Driver subsistence is £1 per day. We'll have to pay about 2p a mile fuel levy. The driver doesn't look wild but he doesn't look mild either, and I can't help noticing the late model Vishnu wired up to the cigarette lighter. I am wondering how much karma I have left.

Karma merchants – gurus, gods, avatars, saviours and the like – seem never to have been in short supply along the Coromandel Coast. The Apostle Thomas came here in AD 56 and was martyred in the course of performing a miracle. South India's oldest temples are here as well as early mosques established by Arab traders. Palm leaf diviners (for about £6, a huge amount) make readings from bundles of ancient *I Ching*-like texts to reveal your fate. Tamils keep the pre-Vedic practice of protecting their villages with huge terracotta horses, gods and goddesses, as well as pampering resident sacred cobras.

The coastal road south through wetlands of rice and palm-topped embankments is, unlike the main road from Madras to Pondy, reassuringly free of vehicle wreckage. Brahminy kites and white-headed eagles soar over paddy fields. Kingfishers peer from telephone wires. We emerge into Tamil Nadu proper at a police check-post and a last chance bar advertising Black Dog Whisky.

This coast is famous for toddy, fermented palm sap. Nadar (Christianised Hindu) tappers shin the 50-foot palmyra and coco palms twice a day to sever growing shoots and attach pots. Tappers 'apologise' to trees with offerings of turmeric and camphor. Placatory rituals ward off snake bite. Night time toddy thieves run the risk of encountering knife blades set into trunks, or finding pots that have been doctored with crushed lizard (diarrhoea) or datura seeds (delirium).

Tappers often scramble across from tree to tree. Near Pondi-cherry, a sprightly 65-year-old who came down from a palm to present me with some of that morning's (acidic, fizzy, surprisingly alcoholic) toddy, had bone-deep cuts where he'd grabbed at saw edged palm fronds to save himself. The manager standing by said it would have been unfortunate if the old man had fallen to his death, because then the tree would have required a long and costly exorcism.

We follow the narrow-gauge railway to Chidambaram where we stretch our legs by walking around the extraordinary 32-acre temple complex with its four immense ceremonial gateways. Here are some of the greatest examples of Chola stone carving and bronze work. And here come holy men from Central Casting, adept camera spotters all, demanding payment for the slightest levelling of a lens. Temple women spread bright washing on the stone courtyards. Oily priests and guides circulate like sucker fish. All life is here. Above all, here are the 1,000-year-old bronzes of dancing Shiva and Parvati.

'Stop!' commands Bettina. Our driver parks in the shade of a tamarind. We have just overtaken a couple of cyclists almost hidden under loads of pots and pans. These men go from village to village buying brass utensils for scrap and selling new stainless steel and aluminium. We wave them down. Bettina swoops. Half an hour later we are on our way with a load of old brass. We pay the pleased dealers £2.40 per kilo for hand-beaten water and milk vessels.

New acquisitions clonking, we make a sharp turn along a road that leads to a run-down settlement my map identifies as Tranquebar – none other than Elvis' fabled 'place where the waves sing.'

We drive under a dilapidated baroque stone arch that bears the date 1792 and the Danish Royal insignia.

Beside a dusty avenue of what had once been fine colonial houses is a Lutheran church, across a neglected *maidan*, a sea-eroded fort. Across the street a curious silver painted concrete bust of a plump man in a periwig sits under a striped sun umbrella. Nearby, flaking notices exhort 'Jesus came into the world to save sinners' and 'Fear of the Lord is the beginning of wisdom.'

Tranquebar was founded in 1620 when the king of Tanjore rented land to the Danes and gave them permission to build a fort. After 160 years during which Tranquebar grew into a busy port and nurtured the first Protestant missions to India, the colonists were expelled by Haidar Ali and the British took over at the beginning of the 19th century. The coming of the railway and the erosion of the shallow coastline, large vessels have to anchor a mile or more out to sea, ensured Tranquebar's demise. These days the population is about 2,000, half Hindu and the rest more or less evenly divided between Christians (Lutherans, Anglicans and Catholics) and Muslims.

A barefoot six-year-old called Deva waylays us on the shimmering walk to the fort and gives us a smile and a sea-shell for one rupee. At the fort, an old man unrolls a scrap of rag and reveals a collection of Danish bronze coins. What about gold? Not in his lifetime, he says, but his father had told stories of gold on the beach. The old man himself is hoping that one day the Taj Hotel group will turn the fort into a tourist oasis.

The man in the wig is Bartolomäus Ziegenbalg, a German Lutheran missionary who was more or less conned into coming here in 1706 by the king of Denmark. Ziegenbalg had his evangelistic heart set upon darker shores than those of India but, by the king's orders, he was not told where the ship was taking him. Ziegenbalg was a difficult customer himself. An uncertain temper can't have been helped by his constant martyrdom to prickly heat. And he insisted on wearing a black wool overcoat. The Danish Governor of the day felt it necessary to cool his perspiring zealot with a spell in jail.

Returning across the old parade ground, we hear the timid rise and fall of familiar hymns from the Tamil Evangelical Lutheran Church, part of Ziegenbalg's legacy to the Coromandel Coast. He also translated the first Tamil Bible and printed it in Tranquebar – not bad for a man who a few years before had waded ashore thinking he was in Africa.

Not the Done Thing in the North-West Frontier

PAKISTAN 1996

They are among the most hospitable people on earth and would unhesitatingly defend a guest with their lives, but a few things have to be borne in mind if you don't want to end up as a kebab yourself when dining with those fierce tribesmen of the North-West Frontier, the Pathans.

Pathans or, perhaps more correctly, Pashtuns or Pukhtuns fired the romantic imagination of our colonial forebears with their courage and chivalry in battle. The bloody colonial battles (the last one was in 1935) against these tall, swashbuckling warriors of the Pakistan/ Afghanistan border are a much-enjoyed topic of Pathan dinner conversation to this day. Lately, tribesmen have had to make do with their usual interminable blood vendettas and the odd skirmish with customs police, but the male guest – especially if he be British – who can convincingly subscribe to the general nostalgia for such interesting times will be well thought of...until, that is, he makes the fatal mistake of sitting with the soles of his feet exposed, breaking wind or enquiring after the health of his host's wife.

In the North-West Territory, which stretches for 700 kilometres astride the Khyber Pass and is the world's largest autonomous tribal society, when girls reach puberty, they disappear. They remain indoors and if they venture outside, they are veiled from head to toe. The western visitor, no matter how puzzled, should refrain from any enquiry as to where they might be – Pathans are convinced that there can be no such thing as an innocent interest in their womenfolk. The traveller who inadvertently rounds a corner in a mountain settlement and finds himself regarded by a pair of unveiled (or, indeed, veiled) eyes, should look down, cross the street, and get out of that neighbourhood pronto.

The all-enveloping modesty garment of Pathan women, the *burqa* remains so inviolable that, despite general suspicion, it is still a preferred disguise for border-crossing Mujahideen, smugglers – and journalists. Few officials would risk compromising the *nang* (honour) of a tribeswoman by peering beneath her veil and thereby invoking a clan obligation for fatal revenge. 'It is nothing my friend – just *badal*,' Nur Muhammad told me as we sat in his simple home one evening and gunfire cracked back and forth in the hills above the Swat Valley. Here, men and teenagers commonly walk around with World War 2 pistols stuck in their belts and/or AK47s slung over their shoulders. Revenge (*badal*) for real or imagined infringements of family honour is and always has been a national speciality.

The polite male visitor to a Pathan house will rap loudly on the door and yell 'Y'Allah!' to give fair warning that any women in the household should disappear to their quarters. At a meal, compliments about (say) the excellence of the food – which will have been prepared by your host's wife and daughters – are best avoided. Non-Muslim guests will often be given individual plates rather than be expected to share communal dishes. Even so, the usual prohibition about eating with the left hand must be observed. It is not the done thing to refuse food or drink, although it is considered greedy to polish off every last drop or crumb. A host exercising *melmastia* –

the Pathan tradition of hospitality – might well take offence at being pressed to take payment.

According to Nur Muhammad (who might have been joking) the only thing I could do after I'd (God forbid) managed to show him my feet, broken wind at his table, showed an interest in his womenfolk and (almost worst of all) given him a limp handshake, was to go through the ceremony of *nanawatai* – formal public apology and abasement.

'But, truly, friend,' said my attentive host, carefully pouring me another glass of cardamom-scented tea, 'if a stranger came here and performed all these abominations you speak of, I think we would be sure he was a poor madman and not worth the killing.'

Over the Andes
in a Bin-Liner

ANDES 1996

'We and the three kids took to bikes eight years ago because it seemed the only way we could all go on holiday together,' explain Roger Manly and his wife Veronica, super-cyclists from Gissing in Norfolk.

'Sailing took up too much time; motoring was out because the children got car sick. Cycling was cheap and flexible – so we went out and bought four bikes and a kiddy seat and five tickets for a flight from London to Guayaquil.'

The Ecuadorean adventure was the first of many for the Manlys – Veronica and husband, Roger, son James (22), and daughters Ruth (21) and Georgina (11). Since then they have cycled in the Canaries, Gambia, New Zealand, Czechoslovakia, Italy, France, Israel and Cuba. 'We were hooked from the start,' says Roger who, with Veronica, runs the family contract cleaning business. The Manlys reckon to put in about 2,000 miles of pedalling every year. 'We're just potterers – it's the scenery and the people that interest us,' they claim – although they have twice completed the annual London–Paris event, a taxing 250 miles in three days.

'That first holiday was the sort of experience you remember for the rest of your life. There we were, Mum, Dad and the three kids, all wearing black plastic bin-liners and pedalling over the Andes in the pouring rain,' recalls Veronica. Bin-liners, to the Manlys, are an indispensable part of long-distance cycling equipment – the plastic bags can be used for protecting food and clothing and, with a neck-hole, they transform into perfect (disposable and light) cycling capes.

The Manlys usually manage to fit in about four long-distance, ten-day trips a year. Three weeks is, they believe, too long ('you just get jaded'); two weeks' cycling, on the other hand, would probably be 'just right' but is often difficult to fit in with running the business.

'Friends think we're mad,' admits Veronica, 'not just because we are always going off on our bikes to places that many people regard as wild and dangerous, but because we travel really light. There are the bin-liners, of course – we wouldn't be without them because then we can leave behind all other waterproof clothing – but we take only one spare T-shirt between all of us. It has to be a large enough to fit Roger. We take just one face flannel which we all use as a towel. Sounds terribly spartan I know, but providing you are well organised and careful to wash things out properly – and you can hang clothes on the handlebars to dry during the day – it's possible to remain quite civilised.'

Not many long-distance cyclists, Veronica admits, would have such a ruthless approach to luggage as she does. Before a trip she prepares just sufficient rations of toothpaste in foil, cuts the handles off toothbrushes and doles out minimum supplies of medicines. The whole family's washing gear is made to fit into a small plastic envelope.

Veronica is a great believer in honey and super-glue: honey for restoring flagging energy and for applying as an antiseptic, super-glue for just about everything, but especially for cuts and grazes. 'You can stick things back on the bikes with the glue, put a dab on screws that might work loose, and if you come off and graze your knee you can put some honey on first and then a nice tough layer of glue for protection.'

Clearly, the Manlys believe that it's better to travel with not enough stuff than too much: 'Sometimes we have to buy the odd piece of clothing or footwear, but we are always meeting other tourers abroad who admit that they are martyring themselves with excess luggage.'

'The secret of being able to travel really light in strange countries, spend the best part of each day expending energy and sweating, and yet retain a good level of comfort,' says Roger, 'is to organise hotels along the route beforehand. We wouldn't dream of camping out. After all, even so-called four-star hotels in third world countries are incredibly cheap by European standards. They often have rather strange notions about the sort of food to give a family of foreign vegetarians, but it's good for our morale at the end of a day to know we only have to pedal another few miles and then we'll have showers and food and clean beds.'

That Ecuador trip, says Roger and Veronica, might have put the younger Manlys – then 14, 13 and 3 – off cycling for ever. Suitable hotels, especially in the Andes, were far apart. There was strange food to cope with, exhaustion in the thin atmosphere of the Andes, and the inner-city dangers of Guayaquil. The teenagers were at that stage in their lives when they could easily have rebelled against the whole concept of a family cycling holiday, especially one where they were expected to pedal 70 or 80 miles to the next hotel,' admits Veronica.

'Luckily, they seemed to thrive on it – and perhaps because we were careful to make the next trip an 'easy' one, in the Canaries – they've been cycling nuts ever since.'

Veronica had 'just a twinge' of apprehension when the five Manlys claimed their bikes at a run-down airport in the Gambia and suddenly realised that their fellow passengers on the Christmas package flight over had all climbed into air-conditioned buses and disappeared. 'A white family cycling along a pot-holed road and obviously lost, was not an everyday sight on the road to Banjul. There was supposed to be a hotel about six miles away from the airport so we just set off,' recalls Veronica, 'and eventually we landed up in this really awful dump of a place. We just had to make the best of it. There was a local lad who kept pestering us, so we roped him in on the Manly team – told him he had been appointed our official guide.

This had the miraculous effect of turning him from a nuisance to a treasure. We left the so-called hotel and rented a nice bungalow from which we could explore. And we cycled over to our young guide's home village and met his family. Lovely people. Roger and the two older children even made a trip on sandy tracks to Senegal. 'It wasn't lost on the kids, when we flew back with the same package tourists, that we had had a very different experience from them.'

Roger and Veronica's two older children have now left home – James to study art at Goldsmiths' College, London, and Ruth to work as an architectural model maker in Berlin. For Georgina, a student at Brandeston Hall School, her 12th birthday this autumn will mark the end of half-price air-flights. 'So, although we did Cuba earlier this year, we feel we must get in another long-haul trip before the fateful birthday,' says Veronica. 'We've been looking at maps of southern Mexico. Maybe we'll be able to get a cheap package deal to a resort like Cancún - and then we'll just cycle off on our own.'

Roger and Veronica think more children should have the sort of opportunities that their children have enjoyed. They bemoan the lack of safe cycle routes to junior schools, and the consequent lack of a natural introduction to cycling. Schoolchildren, they believe, should be allowed to develop cycling skills. And there's no telling, Veronica and Roger stress, where that could lead: 'Farther down the road they might learn the art of greasing a bike chain with packs of hotel butter – or even of going over the Andes in a bin-liner.'

The Thingummy of Swat

PAKISTAN 1996

A fragment of verse has been jolted loose from my subconscious and now threatens to take over the brain altogether: *who or why or which or what* – I ask myself as I peer through a spattered bus window at a rocky landscape five hours north of Islamabad – *who or why or which or what is the Akond of Swat?*

The what of what? The young man in front who has never ceased, during this crowded, thumping journey, to pop golf ball-sized wads of green tobacco into his mouth and spit with neat precision over a couple of heads and out of the window, turns around and nods. 'Yes. Swati,' he says, pointing at himself. 'Good,' I reply, warily. Have I been talking to myself out loud? How much more humiliating if, rather than rehearsing one of Edward Lear's *Nonsense Poems*, I'd been in the deadly grip of *Moon River*. I focus on the hills above the valley of the River Swat, the meandering orchards of mulberry and apricot, the mud-brick and wood settlements where sheepherders carry AK47s, and where women in tent-like *burqas* disappear into doorways.

This was and is outlaw territory. Already, our outrageously decorated and be-tinselled bus has ventured 70 kilometres beyond the site of the last of the 19th-century British garrisons. We are deep in the homelands of the Pathan tribes of Victorian romance. Once the North-West Frontier of the Indian Empire, it is now the equally unruly borderland of Afghanistan and north-west Pakistan – where 'cousin' and 'enemy' are the same word and 'defence' means smuggling. Pathans of the province, a 700-kilometre strip of mountains straddling the Khyber Pass, now comprise the world's biggest autonomous tribal society. Often tall, sometimes blue-eyed or red-headed, they are famous still for bravery, hospitality and bloody-mindedness.

'Best not go much farther up the valley than the last town on the bus route,' a tourism official in Islamabad had warned, 'because if you accidentally witness a smuggling operation or a tribal squabble…well, let's just say it could have an adverse effect on your holiday.'

The bus grinds on and eventually squeals to a stop in the mud streets of the little town of Madyan. This is as far as it goes. Straight-backed men with woollen blankets thrown over one shoulder and groups of sturdy children seem hardly to notice Bettina and me as we get down. After muggy, suburban Islamabad, the air here at 1,300 metres is like chilled wine. To the north, skeins of cloud scrape up and over the pale heights of Gilgit and Chitral. The town below is jammed into a cleft between mountains from which, joining forces as they emerge and cut through and down, emerge the torrents of the Swat and the Madyan rivers. A shout drifts over from a rocky meadow where boys in baggy brown trousers, embroidered shirts and felt caps are pursuing a furious game of cricket: 'Howzat!'

Bettina, who is made of much sterner stuff than I, goes into a roadside shop and buys a *chappli* kebab. The name means 'shoe.' An intimidating dollop of ground mutton, seethed in grease and accompanied by a floppy disc of naan bread, comes wrapped in a page of the *Frontier Post*.

'Is the Madam liking the food of our people?' I am asked by the proprietor. 'She thinks it is terrific,' I reply, steering Bettina (who is

German and apt to say exactly what she thinks) away down the street. 'Try some of this terrific meat thing,' she says, grimly.

I don't know about the kebab, but the *Frontier Post* is good stuff: tribesmen are literally up in arms at the latest attempts of the Federal government to enforce customs regulations and 'enslave' the province. Interior Minister Naseerullah Babar is a 'Mughal' hatching a conspiracy of revenge on behalf of his forefathers (the last Mughal/ Pathan set-to was about 400 years ago, but never mind) and all loyal tribesmen must defend their traditional employment (smuggling, evidently) even to the extent of taking their case to the UN. It all goes to show, I point out, that a person had better treat cultural matters such as, say, national cuisine (the kebab is gone and we have acquired two alert outriders from the local hound population) with tact. 'It's all part of the Great Game,' I tell Bettina.

Those complex diplomatic and military chess moves whereby Britain closed the northern door of its Indian Empire against Russia during the last century, could still be going on as far as the conversation of old Yusuf the barber is concerned. I discover this when I stop by his shop to buy a razor.

Yusuf sits me down outside – Yusuf's is strictly a one-person establishment – with a cup of cardamom-scented tea and brings out his stock. 'These blades are made in Russia and they are sometimes good ones and mostly bad ones, like their army which our brothers have just defeated in Afghanistan,' he says with an apologetic shrug. 'But these blades are from your country, my friend – Inglistan, ha! ha! – and they are best blades and best soldiers. We have good fights with you!' (The last Imperial Army engagement around here was the Battle of Ambela Pass in 1863, and I don't really want to point out to kindly old Yusuf that Solingen isn't quite in Inglistan – but I do my best to look ambassadorial and enjoy the novelty of meeting an admirer of British cold steel.) And at last, I get to put my question: who, or what, *was* the Akond of Swat?

The Akond – the word means religious teacher – was the Sufi ascetic and anti-British reformer Abdul Ghafoor. He rallied clans against the Imperial power in 1849 and even, briefly, established his own state. Following his death and more unrest, Britain installed the Akond's grandson as the first Wali (ruler) of Swat in 1926.

The First Wali was, according to Yusuf, an ingenious man of delicate feelings. He invented a sling-shot for firing six-inch nails which he himself would operate to execute criminals, and he is remembered for having a man tortured for mistreating a chicken. 'If he took pity on a sinner then he would use four-inch nails,' adds Yusuf with what might be a grin.

If he catches them, either old or young/does he have them chopped in pieces or hung/or shot?/the Akond of Swat?... the good old days ended, they say, when the Second Wali, the Akond's great-grandson, was relieved of sovereignty in 1969. Yusuf, along with a majority of older Swatis, dates the coming of many 'evils' – from customs duties to television soap-opera, female education to duff razor-blades – from then.

While I've been talking to Yusuf, Bettina has been deep in conversation with a grubby and enchanting six-year-old girl who now takes us up a series of steep alleyways to meet her father, Fida Mohammad. Fida's family started letting rooms to travellers (bed and room and spartan necessities still available for less than a quid) in the '70s when the Swat Valley was a kind of Shangri-La for long-distance hippies. Since then, the hippies have fallen off and been replaced by middle class Punjabis and a few mainstream European travellers, most of whom tend to stay at one of the two western-style riverside hotels at the north end of the settlement.

'When the young people first started to come here,' says Fida, 'there was no running water, electricity or toilets. The first earth closet we made for our guests fell in and nearly buried a Dane.' Fida once visited traveller friends in Sweden – and was amazed to discover that not all westerners were dope smoking hippies.

Not to be outdone, Muambar Khan, an older member of Fida's family and the person generally credited with inaugurating Madyan's tourist business, says, 'I have never travelled – people visit me instead.

My good friends Karen and Thomas from England. They came here the first time 27 years ago, and they gave me the idea to make a place to stay for the young travellers.'

Bettina is summoned by Fida's young daughters and disappears into the women's quarters while I go off to see a slim, bearded local resident whose name in Pushtu means 'Light of the Prophet.' 'That's my religious name,' says Michael Tetmark, a 43-year-old ex-builder from Copenhagen who has lived in Madyan for five and a half years. 'I worked with a Pathan fellow in a factory in Denmark,' he explains, 'and through him I became fascinated by the whole race. They are frank and up-front and totally independent and they know how to laugh at themselves. By their example I became interested in and then adopted their religion. This is home. Now, when I go to Denmark to visit my family I can't wait to get back here.'

Michael hopes to marry a local Pathan girl before long, but he admits that the process is highly complicated – even dangerous. Once a Pathan girl reaches puberty she disappears from men's sight, never leaving the women's quarters of her family home except in company of an older male relative. Outside, she wears an enveloping *burqa* and sees the world only through a woven grille.

'So, yes, meeting women can be a bit difficult,' says Michael, which – since I happen to know that Pathan men feel perfectly justified in shooting any stranger who looks at, or even asks after, their womenfolk – strikes me as being an understatement and a half. Pathan women, Bettina tells me as we sit on our earth balcony outside one of Fida's pretty wooden huts watching the day fade on the peaks of Mankial and Falak Sar, are beautiful, playful and as curious as cats. Fida's wife and sisters and an excited collection of girls wanted to run their fingers through her light-coloured hair and could hardly contain their interest in the contents of her makeup bag. Everyone, even the babies, had to have a go with the eye-shadow. 'They peek out from cracks in the shutters and they send the young girls out to spy for them. They know all about you,' she says.

That's a bit worrying. I wonder if Madyan's purdah grapevine knows what happened this morning when I got lost in the alleyways leading down to the main road? Turning a corner by a broken wall I found myself looking into the grey-green eyes of a Pathan woman washing a baby in the yard. Instinctively, with soapy fingers, she started to pull her veil across her face and over her long dark hair, and then gave up the gesture, treating me to a cheeky smile that seemed to say: 'So?'

I had stumbled on down the hill to where the daily bus to Karachi was loading – a bargain 36-hour trip from the Himalayas to the tropics for £6 – wondering if I would be wise to get on.

With Mike and the Nightingales

TUSCANY 1996

Déjà-vu. We are sitting on a wooded hillside with a bottle of wine and looking out at cypresses and vineyards and tiled farmhouses. A hoopoe swoops across. We are only a couple of hours' walk away from the stumbling camcorder legions and bus jams of Florence.

It dawns on me where and when I have seen these blue vistas before – in the Uffizi Gallery, yesterday. In fact, I day-dreamed about walking right into the paintings (*saying don't get up – I'm only passing through* to astounded popes, Madonnas and Venuses) and making for that idyllic Renaissance countryside glimpsed in the backgrounds.

Away from motorways and ribbon development, and looking from the vantage points of traditional ridge and stream-bed routes between villages, the hillsides around Florence seem not to have changed much in the last 500 years. Local boys Giotto and Fra Angelico, and Leonardo da Vinci (who tried out his flying machinery at nearby Fiesole) would probably recognise the place. From our picnic spot I can see a turreted village, far away and half hidden behind hills and umbrella pines, that might well have appeared behind the magnificent nose of Lorenzo de' Medici.

No-neck Lorenzo looked the sort of man to enjoy the sort of lunch we lugged along wooded paths and across broom-scented heaths from the little *alimentari* in the suburb of Settignano. There is something about Tuscany that inspires thoughts of food and drink, and a walk there with my old friend Mike Jarman (in real life with his wife Ann who still runs the Old Fire Engine House restaurant in Ely) certainly had the makings of a classic fat boys' outing.

'Think of it as research,' Mike had said, reaching down a large bottle of wine and making prodigal choices among the local salamis, cheeses, breads and steeped olives. We staggered out with our loot but not before we had topped it off with a fragrant sprig of tomatoes and a few cherries. Fellow walkers, Sandra and Robert Jones (renal nurse and building surveyor respectively) from Wolverhampton, observed as they packed their own more orthodox trekkers' requirements of energy bars and mineral water, that no one would be able to accuse Mike or me of neglecting the growing boy within.

Apart from his nutrition consultancy skills and a keen appreciation of Toots & the Maytals, Mike has sharp eyesight – something that proved significant during our ten-day walk around the north-east of Florence using a tour company's excellent but small-print maps and booklets. We had to watch out for Club Alpini Italiano's little painted waymarkers on trees and rocks. On my own I would have ended up in Yugoslavia.

The first day's 15-kilometre walk took about five hours and was no problem even for dedicated lunchees. We saw orchids, helleborines, asphodels, tassel hyacinth and wild sweet peas. And we startled a deer, found some porcupine quills and heard a pheasant – not bad for Italy, where everything that moves sooner or later gets potted-at (which those planning to clamber through undergrowth during the autumn hunting season should bear in mind).

Some of the Club Alpini routes, overgrown to the point of becoming tunnels, were the vestiges of once-important wheel-rutted stone roads. We found the occasional old stone direction-post. Some tracks, which must have been made for pack animals, took us through long-unpopulated uplands. Generally, it was possible to walk for most of the day without meeting a soul or seeing many signs of habitation. Through this tapestry-like landscape with its classical cypresses and shy, flitting birds, we followed roads that had probably been in use since Roman times.

Our longest walk, the 19 kilometres from Bivigliano to Vicchio, started badly. Descending chestnut coppices above Polcanto, Mike twisted his ankle and I broke a strap on my trekking sandals – at exactly the spot, we found out, where a week before a walker in her seventies had fallen and badly injured a foot. She was extricated by the local fire brigade.

We were luckier. A bit of jury-rigging fixed the sandal and Mike's ankle responded favourably to rest and Chianti in the village bar. We took an ancient trackway to some overgrown walls marked on the map as Comune di Monterotondo and made our way up through old forest to a ruined tower marking the remains of a 13th-century castle. On a narrow path all but closed off by brambles, miles from anywhere, we met an Italian cyclist in full lycra and wrap-around shades who insisted he wasn't lost.

That evening, at the posh Villa Campestri hotel which overlooks the birthplace of Fra Angelico at Vicchio, we were shameless in our enthusiasm for raw porcini (ceps) with finely sliced parmesan and for the chef's special spaghetti with orange and lemon and chilli. Then, at Acone, we sat on Signora Veronica Billi's guest house veranda watching fireflies, listening to nightingales and road-testing her home-made grappa – after which it was surprisingly difficult to say 'red-backed shrike,' one of which had been seen frequenting the bushes outside the bathroom window.

Despite Mike's mapmanship, we got lost on our way down to the Sieve valley. I think we went wrong at the tadpole stream in the chestnut forest (but what do I know?). After barging undergrowth for a few miles, we scraped through hedges into an olive grove and found we had chanced upon a waymark. Then a section of main road provided us with a salutary reminder of the world of traffic before we climbed from Scopeti through trees and fields to Castiglione. At last, passing under a grand and dilapidated gateway and welcomed by two huge yellow-eyed sheepdogs, we came – as once, according to a verse in his *Divine Comedy*, did Dante Alighieri – to the Villa Busini.

Guest rooms at the (13th going on 15th-century) Villa Busini have four-poster beds, stone floors, four feet thick walls and the sort of armoires that could conceal a dead horse or a poker game. Signora Maria-Rosaria de Marco Nicolodi's dining room has ranks of old crested tableware, an odd-man-out Italian Futurist teapot, and 18th-century glasses. We carried out a major evaluation of the Busini wine – now in its second year of production and looking good – and enjoyed Signora Nicolodi's home cooking and the Castiglione olive oil. Looking across the valley from the loggia and the garden's lime and wisteria walks, even Rufina (that undistinguished town) managed, by lavender distance, to resemble a Leonardo sketch. Sandra discovered a passion for weeding. We played billiards. It was hard to tear ourselves away.

Our last serious outdoor lunch was beside some vineyards on the edge of woods on the way to Pontassieve railway station. Swifts and martins were criss-crossing a wide-open sky and we polished off fennel-flavoured salami and grocer's Chianti. It was time to head off down our last hillside and catch the train to Florence.

'And where shall we go for dinner?' Mike had wanted to know.

*

In memory of Mike Jarman
29 March 1945 – 14 March 2021

The Seychelles Treasure

Designer-blue sea is rolling in on whitest white coral sand. Coco palms semaphore lazily in the warm wind. It's just another fashion shoot perfect Monday morning in paradise – until Bob Graf sticks his head out of a flooded tunnel at the top of the beach, whips off his diving mask, and announces: 'It's down there – 150 million dollars' worth of pirate treasure!'

This is Bel Ombre, on Mahé, the biggest of the 115 or so Seychelles islands, smack-dab in the middle of the Indian Ocean and 1,000 miles from anywhere. Bob, from Colorado, and his local helpers start bringing up dynamite-loosened boulders from the far reaches of the tunnel. I escape to the shade of a nearby *takamaka* tree. 'Never mind all those Bounty Bar ads that are filmed around here,' says Bob, fixing me with a believer's gaze, 'the discovery of the treasure is going to make this place more famous than Disneyland.'

I am impressed. The whereabouts of Olivier 'The Buzzard' Levasseur's treasure has been a mystery since 1721 when the pirate captured a Portuguese government ship out of Goa. But I never realised that the sexy Eden of the choc-bar advertisements was a real place, and that one day I would stand (if only my adolescent self could see me now!) beside those curvaceous palms. The mind – I tell Bob as he and his team winch another chunk of granite out of the treasure hole – boggles.

'It sure does,' agrees Bob, hauling on a rope. 'Part of Levasseur's treasure is the Fiery Cross of Goa – gold, diamonds, rubies and emeralds – and carrying it aboard was a job for three pirates.'

Bob's murky tunnel goes straight down for about 30 feet and then branches off another 60 or so. The end of the workings is now directly under a bungalow-sized boulder which Bob believes to be the 'roof' of a treasure cave. Bob and his brother-in-law Gilles Payette alternate one and a half hour shifts working by feel at the end of the narrow tunnel, breathing compressed air through a pipe. I wouldn't go down there, I tell Bob, for ten Fiery Crosses of Goa or even all the Bounty Bars in Christendom.

Bob first became involved with Levasseur's lost hoard when he agreed to inject some cash into a search that had ground to a halt. He was assured, he says, that ten thousand pounds and three weeks' more digging would reveal the treasure. That was seven years ago. How much had Bob's seven years of treasure hunting cost? 'Let's just say a real lot of my money and a real lot of other people's money has disappeared down this hole,' says Bob, 'but my calculations tell me that I'm only six feet from the treasure.'

The presumed author of all this fuss, Olivier Levasseur, a French privateer-turned-pirate known as 'La Buse' – The Buzzard – was the scourge of the Indian Ocean in the first quarter of the 18th century. Captured by a French warship in 1730, the pirate – reputedly a scoundrel of education and refinement – went to the scaffold without ever revealing where he had hidden the great treasure he'd taken from the *Virgem do Cabo*.

Tradition has it that La Buze threw a bundle of papers into the crowd just before he was hanged at Réunion, saying: 'Find my treasure who can!' Bob believes he can. But then, so did the late Reginald

Herbert Cruise-Wilkins who expended his health, his wealth and 27 years of his life without coming up with so much as a doubloon. Reg's son John believes he now knows where the treasure is – and, having fallen out with his erstwhile partner Bob Graf, hopes to secure a government permit to dig on the shore when Bob's licence runs out this year. 'He might find part of the treasure where he's digging,' says John when I speak to him later at the family home overlooking the beach at Bel Ombre, 'but I'm pretty sure that the treasure has been split up. I think I know where it is…'

Contradictory and obscure collections of papers from archives in France, La Réunion and Madagascar, purporting to be the originals or copies of La Buse's bundle could, I think, be seen as revenge rather than legacy. Nevertheless, to the end of his days, ex-Grenadier Guardsman, ex-big game hunter Reg Cruise-Wilkins believed that Levasseur's mare's nest of star-charts, disconnected notes in old French and dozen lines of cryptogram (part of which decodes: 'provoke a certain woman waterlogged') are an elaborate puzzle based on the Twelve Labours of Hercules.

'It was a game devised by Levasseur for his own amusement and for the befuddlement of those he intended to seek the treasure,' was Reg's verdict.

With the first £200 of backers' money, Reg Cruise-Wilkins unearthed an odd-shaped stone which he was sure represented Andromeda chained on the Ethiopian shore. As far as Reg was concerned, this was Exhibit A and he was on the right track. In the event, doing a re-run of all Twelve Labours on the granite coast of Mahé was going to occupy him for the rest of his life. His search would also involve a great deal of dynamite and the resources of more than 500 investors.

The Labours piled up, each excavation yielding, according to Reg, new clues: three stone cannon balls were symbols of the Golden Apples of the Hesperides; a nodule of ironstone shaped rather like an antique sandal was seen as a reference to the one that Jason lost crossing the Anaurus; on a small hill overlooking the bay, the skeleton of a horse 'buried in a peculiar fashion' was a sign for Pegasus, Perseus' winged steed.

Over the years, day-labourers' wages went from £2.20 a month to the same amount per day and, not surprisingly in the absence of the expected finds, some backers turned bolshie. There was even a run-in with the Mahé Public Works Department over the Ninth Labour when Reg took on the Herculean task of blasting into the foundations of the main coastal road to seek the girdle of Hippolyta, Queen of the Amazons.

Years after his father's death, John has admitted: 'what drives me is hunger to prove my father right – it's not the money.'

Bob Graf also gives the impression of a man driven by something other than financial gain. He is an adherent of the Greek mythology theory and sees the rocky foreshore of Bel Ombre as having been modified by Levasseur into a classical theme park guarding the treasure. 'He (Levasseur) wants me to go into the treasure room through the front door of his construction,' says Bob, 'and I'm going in by the laundry chute instead. I could simply dynamite a way in from the top but that would destroy everything. It would just be greed.'

Separately, I ask John and Bob if they have ever considered that they might simply be mistaken – that there might be no riddle based on Greek mythology? – no hundred million quid's worth of treasure? It's not, I realise, the sort of doubt your committed treasure-hunter willingly entertains.

'Levasseur's treasure, which my father saw as the Golden Fleece, has always been there in my life,' says John Cruise-Wilkins simply. He then produces what he considers to be a major piece of supporting evidence – an ancient ebony and ivory domino piece with six and two dots. It was found during his father's last dig.

The number 62, says John, corresponds with a 'crucial' angle mentioned in the documents and indicates where the treasure will be found (but what, I wondered, if the 62 turned out to be a 26 or even just 2 and 6?).

Bob Graf, who also believes the domino was planted by Levasseur as an important clue, walks me a few yards along the rock-piled high-tide line and points to an overhang of weathered granite. 'Doesn't that look like a buzzard?' he asks.

Feeling like Polonius in Scene 2, Act 3 of *Hamlet* when he has to agree with his gloomy Prince that a passing cloud does, indeed, resemble a camel, then a weasel, then a whale, I squint manfully until I think I can make out, among the furrows and gougings, a curved beak and part of a back-turned wing. I ought to mention that it could equally well be a dodo or the *Winged Victory of Samothrace* or the bumper of a 1950s Buick.

Bob next points out a curlicued, natural-looking rock formation. 'Er, a big pineapple?' I venture. 'Medusa, the snake-haired Gorgon!' announces Bob. Another pile of granite jutting out of the sand, he says, is our old friend Pegasus. For the life of me, I say, I cannot make out a horse, winged or plain. 'Nor could I until I realised that this Pegasus is upside-down!' cries Bob.

Maybe I am, after all, acquiring a treasure hunter's slant on the world because, on the way back across the island to the capital, Victoria, I can't help noticing Willy the taxi-driver's Medusa-esque dreadlocks. And then there's the reggae gospel song thumping over the car radio with the refrain: 'and de rock shall be cleaved...'

Willy listens patiently to my goings-on about the Great Pirate Treasure Mystery, and then says, 'Yeah, I been hearing a lot of that for years. I daresay some of it might come up true. But them horse's bones Mr Wilkins, rest his soul, found didn't belong to no famous old Greek animal. That one used to be a favourite of Mister Savy and its name was Sap-sap.'

Real Gauchos,
Wrong Trousers

These are exactly the right trousers. Sky-blue, wide-legged, with
intricate pleats and natty rows of pink embroidered tulips down the
seams, they are real gaucho *bombachas*. I suspect I have been looking
for them all my life. For a mere eight quid in Uruguayan pesos I am
about to become a South American cowboy.

We are all cowboys or cowgirls at heart – at least we were until
Time bushwhacked us with mortgages, soft furnishings and pension
plans. But it never really dies, that old leathery itch for the open range.
Why else would I be here in the middle of the Uruguayan pampas
when I am supposed to be refining my tango twirls in the salons
of Montevideo?

That, of course, is another story altogether. Anyway, here I am
sitting next to a beer in a general store-cum-bar beside a dirt road
not far from a river known as the Escape-From-Here-Who-Can and
I'm idly contemplating a dusty shelf of cheap cowboy duds.

It has to be workaday, inexpensive stuff, this clobber. Gauchos
of the pampas are not like their rich cowboy cousins in the far north.
No pick-up trucks, no Marlboro ad chic for them. Poverty has saved
them from large hair and line-dancing.

The old gaucho in the corner, however, isn't feeling poor. Perching unsteadily on his chair at the bar and waving a handful of banknotes to show me he is a man of at least temporary substance, Santos Vega Leal offers me a drink. Santos' horse, parked outside, looks in through the doorway occasionally. Santos' pet terrier sits on his lap and shows teeth whenever a larger dog wanders in. Santos is wearing his best pay-day outfit of boots, *bombachas,* red-trimmed cloak and beret. A rawhide whip dangles from his wrist.

Originally, gauchos like Santos were a complex but distinct *mestizo* conjunction of Spanish migrant, African slave and native South American. They were useful to encroaching landowners and cattle agents in clearing the ranges of Charrúa and Chaná Indians. On the banks of the Salsipuedes River, the one near my general store and bar, the last of the Rio Negro Indians were slaughtered.

On the plains, Voodoo (West African *Candomblé*) went hand in hand with Christian observance and the stately Catalonian Sardana was danced in eerie groves of *ombú* trees. Gauchos were famously generous and infamously quick to take offence. They rode barefoot and flung the rawhide Indian *bolas* to bring down wandering cattle and *ñandu,* the native emu. Barefoot riding was going out when *bombachas* were coming in around the middle of the 19th century.

Following the Crimean War, a huge supply of redundant Zouave uniform trousers – blue, red or white according to which battalion of French North African light infantry they had graced – were dumped on the civilian market. Before that, gauchos – if the early paintings in Montevideo's Blanes Museum are anything to go by – wore white canvas flares with (get them!) lacy bell-bottoms.

Uruguayans eat more beef and drink more *maté* (the hot and bitter tea of *Ilex paraguariensis*) than the people of any other nation. And, among Uruguayans, gauchos have always been the biggest consumers of both. The Spanish word for meat – *carne* – to a gaucho simply indicates beef. Sheep meat is a poorly regarded substitute, chicken unthinkable, vegetables a rumour, salads non-existent. If you are dining with gauchos, you will wait in vain for that nice little radicchio and sorrel number with the sprigs of rocket and the oh-so-important balsamic dressing.

What you get is meat. Joints of seared *carne* are passed around the company who, traditionally, will be squatting on their haunches around a wood fire. Protocol dictates you grip the meat with your teeth and saw off a generous portion with a knife before handing it along.

Gauchos always employed their knives, *facóns*, carried behind and thrust into tinselled, wide belts, for dispatching cattle and often each other. The *facón* is also a castrating tool, abridger of dogs' tails and handy toothpick.

And if a gaucho, taking pity on a poor unequipped gringo, say, offers you the use of such a knife to carve yourself a hunk from the barbecue, it would be as well to remember that you are being accorded a great and unrefusable honour.

To be ungracious about such an offer would be as bad as aspersing a man's horse, something I did the other day, so help me, to the first gaucho I ever met. He is known as Cinnamon (*Canella*), and his pony is a beauty called Dove (*Paloma*). Canella works at a small *estancia* near the Talita River just north of Montevideo. A few days ago, when he led out Paloma for me and cinched up the saddle of raw sheepskin, I made some daft remark along the lines of 'well, at least I'm going to be falling off in style, ho ho.'

Born in the saddle, Canella had naturally assumed that, since I was as rich in grey hairs as he, I would be a similarly experienced horseman. From my remark he would have been forced to conclude I was anticipating faults in the sweet-natured Paloma.

Canella was mollified I think when, out on the range, it soon became clear just how much of a tyro his charge was – one who didn't even know how to steer a pony by a hand on the neck for goodness' sake! He sidled up at a tricky moment when it looked as if Paloma and I would be joining an absconding band of emus and advised politely: 'Señor, she does not understand the pull on the mouth. Maybe she think you want her stand on her back legs like for the rodeo.'

After that I did my best to treat Paloma like a lady. Canella put aside my silly remark and settled into the comfortable role of guide instructor. He showed me hawks and partridge and hares and the dried-out cadavers of armadillos. We rode back towards the setting sun, arriving at the Estancia Doña Yita just as small parrots were settling down for the night in their communal nests in the eucalypts.

Marta Aramburu Rivero, the owner, told me that her 800-hectare *estancia* had been derelict on and off for about 200 years because it was too small to employ enough gauchos to protect itself from the depredations of much larger neighbours.

Cattle stealing has declined in recent years along with the ranch business generally, but the tradition of lawlessness on the wide-open prairies has never died out completely. Butch Cassidy and the Sundance Kid hung out around here when they were on the run at the turn of the last century, and in the 1960s and '70s leftist *Tupamaros* used the interior as a base for robbing banks and harassing the authoritarian right-wing establishment of the day.

Some Uruguayan *estancias* benefitted from the political struggles and chaos in neighbouring Argentina during the 1970s and '80s. Well-to-do Argentinians, fearful of kidnap by left-wing urban guerrillas at home, took refuge for holidays and weekends as paying guests across the River Plate. At the same time, Argentine Marxist guerrillas, *Montoneros*, in a situation that surely had more Groucho than Karl about it, would be chilling-out at the same *estancias*, pretending to be tourists.

And, now I come to think of it, the Marx Brothers would have recognised the set-up in my general-store-cum-bar in the middle of nowhere: the bar, when I went out back to change, had contained only Paula, who runs the place, her new baby Maria, old Santos and several dogs. Now it is full of young cowboys. They clump around the bar and touch their hats respectfully to me and with wide grins applaud the new blue *bombachas*.

But then the two Cecilias come in – my friend Cecilia Regules, who owns the nearby *estancia*, Las Cañadas, where I am staying, and her six-year-old daughter. At dinner last night Little Cecilia gave me a lingering hug while whispering in my ear that she wanted me to have her *piojos*. I was touched – until I looked up the word later and found it meant lice. She now beams me the most exquisite smile in the world. I forgive her the nits. Big Cecilia isn't smiling. She looks me up and down and says crushingly, 'Tulips! No way, José – I'm not taking you back to the farm in those!'

A Gannet in the Garfagnana

My gourmet trip gets off to a – well, actually not bad – start with Ryanair's *collation en box de cardboard* which includes two sorts of cheesy spread, a Spam-inspired article, cellophaned biscuits and a tub of jam. OK, if a little *cher*, but what the hell! I'm on my way to Tuscany to be wined and dined at their annual Chestnut Festival by the Garfagnana Chestnut Growers' Association, so I'm in foodie mode. I lash out on a mini wine. A quick twist and a surprisingly alert Merlot springs from its plastic prison like a neglected genie. If it did the right thing and granted me a wish, I'd be tempted to ask for my seven quid back.

The Garfagnana is an easy drive from the airport at Pisa; just follow the Serchio Valley road winding north above Lucca. Very soon you find yourself looking up at snowy heights and the bosky slopes that are part of Europe's most extensive chestnut forest. We pass maize fields, straggling at this time of the year, and farmhouses with stacks of wood under the eaves. Skeletal black persimmon trees still hold last season's startling orange globes. The smell of wood smoke is coming through the dashboard air-blower.

This north-western corner of Tuscany bounded by the Apennines and the Alpi Apuane, is not on the usual tourist menu. In the past it was known chiefly for being a bandit-heavy stage on the pilgrim way between the St Bernard Pass and Rome. And Ludovico Ariosto wasn't impressed either. Renaissance courtier and author of *Orlando Furioso* (the very long poem that gave European literature the nudge it needed to go in a more confessions-of-a-celebrity-love-rat direction), Ludovico took one shuddering look at the Garfagnana before scurrying back whence he had lately come.

What with the Eek! factor of unwashed bandits, altogether too much porridge and who knows what other upsets, it seems he had plumb forgotten that the Duke of Ferrara had just appointed him the region's governor. Not for the first time (as history tells but space, alas, prevents us from examining here) Ludovico had some explaining to do. Suffice it to say that he once excused himself from a diplomatic mission to Hungary on the grounds that he was in the grip of a fever; he didn't mention that her name was Alessandra Benucci.

For the peasants, if not their fastidious governor, however, the Garfagnana was a blessed land where each *Castanea sativa* tree could provide the staff of life (porridge, essentially) for 1,000 years. In fact, the chestnut was central to the local economy until well after World War 2, as Councillor Ivo Poli, head of the Association of Chestnut Growers explains when I catch up with him in the pretty medieval town of Castelnuovo.

Bunting spans the flagstones around the medieval fortress that is now the Town Hall. Cold winds are coming down from the Alpi Apuane. Drill squads of boys and girls wearing tights of faux-Renaissance motley are tossing and catching flags in the square. This annual winter festival celebrates all things chestnutty – chestnut pancakes, chestnut polenta and chestnut ice cream through to, yes, chestnut beer. It doesn't stop at chestnuts, of course. The festival is a comprehensive gannet-fest embracing olive oil, cheese, and those particular gifts to mankind that come courtesy of the noble pig.

According to Ivo Poli, the last three months of a true Garfagnana porker's life must be spent nosing around in chestnut woods. 'Then they are happy and they get four fingers of fat on their back and that makes them delicious.' What, I wonder, would be the Italian for 'a hooray/boo situation'? Speaking for myself, I would feel at least a tweak of paranoia if some cannibal benefactor kept sending me down the pub and then enquiring about how my beer-gut was coming along.

But I don't want to dwell upon the inevitable link between salami and death because I am setting out in search of Castelnuovo's very own Godfather of Grub, Andrea Bertucci and his legendary Osteria Vecchio Mulino. Sleet is starting to enfilade the big door of the Town Hall as I leave but the Old Mill is not many steps away. Inside, it has the scruffy charm of one of those pre-EU Irish pubs that also functioned as grocer's, post office, and repository of out-of-date calendars of tractors.

The difference is that in this parallel gastronomic universe lunch will not consist of dodgy soda bread and packet soup with a subtle hint of paraffin. With anticipation I slip into a corner beside a sack of beans at the single long table.

The Old Mill is a little theatre-in-the-round of food, and proprietor Andrea is the big (in every sense) lead. He's flamboyantly wielding a claymore of a knife and using it to hand round slices from a Mortadella about the size of himself. The Biggest Sausage in the World is good stuff, going towards the platonic ideal, I would say, and Andrea's other food booty is all around the walls and ripely dangling from the ceiling. There are Serrano and Prosciutto hams with handwritten labels. Of regional salamis we have the complete *megillah*.

There cannot be many better ways of spending the best part of a sleety afternoon thus, working through the 15-euro lunch at Andrea's place. With a carafe of Chianti thrown in, this includes (Linda McCartneyites can look away now): cuts from the salamis and the raw hams overhead, local red polenta with pheasant sauce and goats' cheese, a savoury tartlet, suckling pig, tongue with anchovies and capers, beef carpaccio with porcini mushrooms, Biroldo, the Garfagnana blood pudding, back fat (lardo) of the Cinta Senese breed of pig, and pecorino old and young from local hill-farms.

If I've missed anything here, it's because my host keeps bringing new goodies. Andrea, I suspect, wants to make all customers as sleek as he is. Again, he leaps up with a cry and this time it's to bring over a chunk of crisp piglet covered in leek preserve. Andrea the Shaman has turned me into a shoal of piranha. Obediently, I chomp.

By virtue of my perch on the end of the table, I am now one of a family of 13, including grandparents and beaming babies. We are a noisy lot except for the young engaged couple sitting even closer together than the rest of us. She carefully fills his glass with a gesture from a scene you might see on a Greek vase. A little too boisterously, perhaps, we drink to the goddess and her chosen dark-eyed shepherd boy.

After Andrea's alleged 'lunch' and an evening's digestive stroll in the town among barrels of roasting chestnuts and the lamp-lit stalls serving nut pancakes, I think I might be ready to give up on this eating lark altogether. But it's a line of business in which you have to be strong, so the next morning I find myself sitting down to a seven-course, all-chestnut dinner.

Ivo is to blame. He brought me here to Giordano and Maurizio's restaurant Il Pozzo in the mountain village of Pieve Fosciana for what he warns will be the definitive chestnut experience.

He wasn't kidding. Chestnuts – we have them every which way: with milk, roasted pig bones, wine, sausage, and with rosemary and ricotta and with orange zest and in the form of (Giordano's speciality this) mousse. We work our way through to chestnut grappa and if they made them, we'd be puffing on chestnut cigars.

Somewhere along the way we even got stuck into that famous chestnut porridge which, I have to admit, turns out to be remarkably good stuff. Those medieval Garfagnana peasants knew what they were about. Ludovico should have tried it with *lashings* of cream.

*

In memory of Andrea Bertucci
1964–2022